T0278426

Cambridge Elements ≡

Elements in Publishing and Book Culture
edited by
Samantha Rayner
University College London
Leah Tether
University of Bristol

YA ANTHOLOGIES

Amplifying Voices, Building Community

Melanie Ramdarshan Bold
University of Glasgow

CAMBRIDGE
UNIVERSITY PRESS

CAMBRIDGE
UNIVERSITY PRESS

Shaftesbury Road, Cambridge CB2 8EA, United Kingdom

One Liberty Plaza, 20th Floor, New York, NY 10006, USA

477 Williamstown Road, Port Melbourne, VIC 3207, Australia

314–321, 3rd Floor, Plot 3, Splendor Forum, Jasola District Centre,
New Delhi – 110025, India

103 Penang Road, #05–06/07, Visioncrest Commercial, Singapore 238467

Cambridge University Press is part of Cambridge University Press & Assessment,
a department of the University of Cambridge.

We share the University's mission to contribute to society through the pursuit of
education, learning and research at the highest international levels of excellence.

www.cambridge.org
Information on this title: www.cambridge.org/9781108725620

DOI: 10.1017/9781108663687

When citing this work, please include a reference to the DOI 10.1017/9781108663687

First published 2024

A catalogue record for this publication is available from the British Library.

ISBN 978-1-108-72562-0 Paperback
ISSN 2514-8524 (online)
ISSN 2514-8516 (print)

YA Anthologies

Amplifying Voices, Building Community

Elements in Publishing and Book Culture

DOI: 10.1017/9781108663687
First published online: June 2024

Melanie Ramdarshan Bold
University of Glasgow

Author for correspondence: Melanie Ramdarshan Bold,
melanie.ramdarshanbold@glasgow.ac.uk

ABSTRACT: Despite their long publishing history, anthologies have received little scholarly attention. However, they play an important role in collecting, and reflecting upon, voices and identities that have all-to-often been on the fringes of publishing. This Element explores the sociocultural functions of anthologies in relation to discussions around exclusion/ inclusion in the publishing industry. Focusing on YA anthologies, using a case study of *A Change Is Gonna Come* anthology (2017), this Element argues that the form and function of anthologies allows them to respond to and represent changing ideas of socially marginalised identities. In *A Change Is Gonna Come*, this medium also affords BPOC authors a platform and community for introspection and the development of both individual and collective identities. Beyond merely introducing writings by socially marginalised groups, this Element contends that YA anthologies embody a form of literary activism, fostering community-building and offering a means to circumvent obstacles prevalent in publishing.

KEYWORDS: young adult fiction, authorship, anthologies, diversity/ inclusion, publishing/publishers

ISBNs: 9781108725620 (PB), 9781108663687 (OC)
ISSNs: 2514-8524 (online), 2514-8516 (print)

Contents

1 Anthologising Anthologies

Anthologies can be powerful tastemakers; historically, they have been responsible for creating and standardising a national canon of literature, whilst offering more opportunities for an emerging society of readers (Price, 2000; Benedict, 2018). However, more recently, anthologies have challenged notions of canonisation by promoting new and underrepresented authors and stories (Lauter, 2004; Damrosch & Spivak, 2011). Despite their long publishing history and the importance of anthologies in canonisation, tastemaking, and challenges to both canonisation and tastemaking, little scholarly research has been written on this area. In fact, only two core monographs focusing on anthologies have been published to date: *Making the Modern Reader: Cultural Mediation in Early Modern Literary Anthologies* (2018) by Barbara M. Benedict and *The Anthology and the Rise of the Novel* by Leah Price (2000). It is no surprise that the authors of these books address this fact. For example, Price (2000) argues, 'although literary critics spend at least as much time quoting out of context as do literary anthologists, the profession that teaches anthologies has provided few theories of the genre' (p. 2). This Element contributes to the theorisation of anthologies by building upon such studies and bringing discussions firmly into twenty-first-century Young Adult Fiction (YA) publishing. Primarily, this Element is concerned with the transformative role that Western Anglophone anthologies play in challenging the established norms of YA authorship and the representation of socially marginalised groups.

Outline of Element

This chapter provides a brief history of how the anthology, as a form, developed alongside the changes in the publishing industry, copyright law, and authorship during the Early Modern period.[1] It examines how modern

---

[1] Due to space constraints, this Element will not discuss the earliest instances of anthology-like collections in ancient civilisations, such as classical Chinese poetry collections (e.g. the Shih Ching) and Greek epigram collections (see: Baumbach et al., 2010; Yu, 2018). This Element will focus on Western Anglophone anthologies.

anthologies began to focus on authors from socially marginalised groups and how this contributed to the development of inclusion, diversity, and identity-formation, challenged the canon, and continue to do so to this day. These conversations and histories are contextualised within the field of young adult literature (YA) in Chapters 2 and 3. By analysing the history of anthologies, this Element identifies patterns of exclusion that have persisted over time. These patterns often have deep historical roots. Recognising these patterns is essential for addressing ongoing issues of exclusion in contemporary literature and working towards greater inclusivity. Chapter 2 details the development of YA anthologies, using a selection of key YA Anthology texts to understand and map the evolution of this genre (and the subgenres within it). This history focuses on: Queer YA; Race and Ethnicity; Bodies and Minds; and Activism. It analyses anthologies that centre on, or at least include, authors from socially marginalised groups. The field of YA often tackles a wide range of social issues, including racism, sexism, homophobia, ableism, classism, and more (Cart, 2016). Analysing the representation of these marginalised identities in YA therefore offers valuable insights into the ways in which exclusionary dynamics operate within the field. However, most of the examples discussed in Chapters 2 are US-centric. This is because the United States (US) has a very large and influential YA market, which impacts reading cultures across the world (including the UK) (Jenkins & Cart, 2018; Ramdarshan Bold, 2021). Anthologies are, and have historically been, a communal endeavour. From the collective nature of manuscript coteries, which made up early miscellanies and were the forbearer to the more formal anthologies in the eighteenth century, to the anthologies we know today: anthologies showcase the relationship between the writer, booksellers/publishers, and reader (Benedict, 2003). Chapter 3 explores this relationship to understand if and how YA anthologies are fostering a space where contributors can develop individual and collective identities. Importantly, especially to counter the US-centricness of YA, Chapter 3 presents a case study of a British YA (UKYA) anthology, situating the discussion within a British context. This helps us reflect upon and understand what British inclusive youth literature tells us about the UK today.

Form and Function

An anthology is a compilation of different works by various authors, often centred around a different theme, genre, time period, or country/culture (Price, 2000; Di Leo, 2004; Benedict, 2018). The exact definition of what an anthology is varies: neither publishers nor scholars have settled on uniform terminology. William Germano, the former vice president and publishing director of Routledge, suggests two categories: collections and anthologies. This is based on the level of editorial activity each requires. Collections, Germano (2001) argues, are 'gatherings of new or mostly new writing'; this requires the editor to seek contributors, and commission work from their networks. Anthologies, on the other hand, are 'previously published or mostly previously published work', which means editors collate 'the best of what has been thought and said' (p. 121): this reflects the original distinction, which will be detailed later in this chapter. Prescott (2016, p. 565) describes the latter, where the short story may have been published in a magazine or another publication, as the 'standard route'. Conversely, he calls anthologies that bring new writing to the fore, including through prizes, 'adventurous'. 'Adventurous' anthologies, or collections that feature new writing and genre or popular fiction, can be seen as prompt and opportunistic forays into the market, while collections of 'previously published or mostly previously published work' strive to make enduring and impactful contributions to the field, regardless of their commercial success. This Element focuses on the 'adventurous' anthologies, the collections of new writing, and what this means not only for the genre but for the publishing industry in general. It looks specifically at curated collections that bring together the work of several authors (instead of the collected works of one author). For example, Chapter 3 presents an illuminating exploratory case study focused on the *A Change Is Gonna Come* YA anthology, which was published by Stripes/Little Tiger in 2017, specifically to tackle issues of exclusion in British publishing and writing. This anthology serves as an exemplar of how these collections can be catalysts for profound change, not only within the literary landscape but also within society at large.

Related to the topic of this Element are the numerous studies, in recent years, that have argued how exclusionary the English-language publishing industries are (Saha, 2017; Ramdarshan Bold, 2019a, 2019b; So, 2020). In the UK and the US, publishing is dominated by global, transmedia conglomerates that favour certain genres, languages, and types of authors, and those who do not fall within certain categories have found themselves writing and publishing on the margins. Historically, anthologies have been central in instituting a restricted canon. Jarrell (1994, p.9) observes that 'Any anthology is, as the dictionary says, a bouquet – a bouquet that leaves out most of the world's flowers'. Anthologies, like bouquets, are carefully curated to display the individual stories or poems within the collection but ultimately reflect the choice and tastes of the selector. Consequently, 'anthologies are more than a referendum. They determine not simply who gets published or what gets read, but who reads, and how' (Price, 2000, p.3). For example, when considering the creation of an African American literary canon and the role of African American literature in creating counternarratives, Henry Louis Gates, Jnr contends, 'a well-marked anthology functions in the academy to create a tradition, as well as to defend and present it' (Gates, 1992, p.31). Anthologies can, therefore, have a valuable role in expanding the circulation and awareness of literature by authors from socially marginalised groups, particularly racialised (i.e. Black, Indigenous, and People of Colour) authors;[2] literature that

---

[2] No terminology used to describe people's 'race' and ethnicity is perfect, and language is evolving continuously. Throughout this Element, Black, Indigenous, and People of Colour (BIPOC) and Black and People of Colour (BPOC: UK terminology) are used as general terms to describe people, specifically authors, from racially marginalised groups. As the author of this Element, I acknowledge the problems associated with using acronyms to capture the complex histories and cultures of racially marginalised people. I also acknowledge that people within these groups have distinct and different identities, and that this also differs across national contexts; the terms are used as a social identity that reflects shared cultures and experiences. Black refers to people from the African diaspora. Black is a distinct category from People of Colour because Black people face higher levels of discrimination than any other racialised group. Wherever possible, precise terminology to describe the specific ethnicity of a person or group will be used.

has been historically overlooked by traditional publishing in the UK (and the US). The open and flexible nature of the format means that readers can approach the content from different points and make different connections between the texts. Bond (2019) argues that this makes anthologies a participatory genre and, as such, can be 'vehicles for collective action' (p.168). Consequently, this Element explores the social and cultural functions of anthologies in relation to discussions around exclusion and inclusion in the publishing industry, and charts how this has developed over the years.

A [Brief] History of Anthologies

During the Early Modern period, there was a significant movement in literature: from the oral tradition to print culture in Europe, and books as an elite product to a mass-produced commodity (Benedict, 2003). Anthologies were a part of this shift. Early anthologies – or miscellanies, as they were more accurately called – were not collected by the quality, or even the content, of the work, but by convenience. Miscellanies have a potted history: booksellers often pieced together remaindered materials – poems, sermons, plays – loosely group by genre or theme. There was no formal structure or formula to these loosely grouped collections: in fact, they were quite haphazard, including anything from two to a hundred pieces of work from one, or dozens of authors (Benedict, 2003). These roughly assembled pieces were often in response to the trends and fashions of the day to provide 'variety and novelty' (Price, 2000, p.4). The haphazard miscellanies developed into something more commercial after the post-Interregnum society: there was a growing number of writers and readers, and booksellers decided to capitalise on this with printed anthologies. The booksellers were involved in most aspects of the production process: from initiating the process to distributing and adverting the works. Consequently, Benedict (2003) argues that 'the story of the anthology in the period is very much a story of booksellers' innovation' (p.36).

Booksellers in the mid-sixteenth century created a more commercial market-place, which was a result of the rise in literacy and a change in the religious and political climate (Feather, 2006). The term 'publisher', as we know it now, was not used until the eighteenth century, and even in the eighteenth century it was used to describe someone who arranged and financed the project. During this period, the term 'bookseller' was more commonly used because 'publishing' was seen as an additional activity for members of the book trade (Sher, 2006). The advent of copyright legislation engendered the advent of 'publishers' because it reduced the importance of both bookbinders and printers, which enabled the publisher – or the bookseller as they were known then – to become the dominant figure in the book trade (Patterson, 1968). These booksellers – the early publishers – hired other people to write and print books, so they had to make money elsewhere. The anthology was a genre that profited from copyright. Booksellers could collect works for which they owned the copyright, and repackage them as a new book to maximise profit (Benedict, 2003). Additionally, fashionable poets – such as Samuel Johnson and John Gay – were recruited as editors to confer prestige on publications. Booksellers began targeting different audiences with different formats: books were kept at a high price, for wealthy readers, while lower-cost pamphlets were aimed at less wealthy readers (Benedict, 2003).

Anthologies have, historically, had a synergic function; it was, and still is to some extent, a genre in which booksellers/publishers, authors, and readers could collaborate (McKenzie, 2002). Benedict (2003, 2015) and Crawford (2023) have argued that the collaborative form and function of anthologies can liberate them from rigid structures. As Benedict (2015) argues, '[anthologies] pull language out of legal frameworks and decentralize literary culture [. . .] by their subversive deferral of a central authority' (p.221). In fact, Benedict (2015) extols the unifying role of the bookseller:

> Literary anthologies influenced writers as much as readers, and made booksellers participants in the creation of culture [. . .] They are partly responsible, in fact, for binding a fractured society by making easily available a shared body of various texts, for England at the Restoration of the monarchy in 1660, following the divisive English Civil War (1642–49) and Interregnum, was a diverse society [. . .] The late seventeenth- and eighteenth-century anthology helped to unify British society and to induct new classes of readers – women, the under-educated – into literary culture. (p.36)

The literary anthology genre grew and developed during the long eighteenth century to the early Victorian period. The anthology, which offered literary variety, was one of the most important genres for readers and writers by the eighteenth century (Benedict, 2003). After a period of censorship, there was a growing number of readers, across social class and genders, in Restoration England (MacLean, 1994). By the end of the eighteenth century, anthologies were influential in establishing a British literary canon (Bonnell, 2008). There was a boom in literary anthologies, in the UK, in the mid-nineteenth century. These anthologies, a mix of short stories and poetry, were typically gift books aimed at young women. Such gift books also included annual anthologies, which were important for genre development and raising the visibility of topical writing. These annuals, and short story magazines in general,[3] were an important source of income for women writers in the nineteenth century (Prescott, 2016). Additionally, literature, as a field of study, was introduced into the British school classroom in the late nineteenth century; so, this period saw anthologies, as a classroom textbook, flourish. In the UK, literary anthologies have been used in mass education more widely since the twentieth century (Banta, 1993). Anthologies based around a specific theme or time period have been used, by secondary and higher educators, to develop pupils/students reading range. For example, the English Association[4] published its own anthologies – *English Short Stories of Today*, to showcase prominent authors – such as H. G. Wells and John Galsworthy – to school pupils. The inclusion of postcolonial authors, such as Chinua Achebe and V.S. Naipaul, in the fourth series published in 1976, showed the new developments in canon-formation (Prescott, 2016).

'Modern' anthologies proliferated in the mid-twentieth century; however, there was an uncertainly around their status. Concerns focused on 'the challenges of narrative experimentation and modernist innovation' (Prescott, 2016, p.570). In the introduction to *Modern English Short Stories 1930–1955* (1956), editor Derek Hudson concluded, 'this much is certain – that

---

[3] Such as, the short-lived, *The Yellow Book*.

[4] The English Association was established in 1906 to promote English Studies in schools. Their first anthology was published in 1939.

these stories do not derive from a dying art' (p.xiv). Christopher Dolley, who would take over from Allen Lane as Chairman and Managing Director of Penguin Books in 1969, echoed these sentiments over a decade later. In his editorial foreword to the *Penguin Book of English Short Stories*, Dolley (1967, p.5) emphasises the focus on modern writing:

> The aim of this collection is to appeal to the reader at large.
> No attempt has been made to conduct a historical survey of
> the English short story, and the collection starts in the mid
> nineteenth century, from which date the short story devel-
> oped as a recognizable genre.

Furthermore, he stresses the healthy nature of the genre, 'The short story still flourishes.' The disquiet about the genre is reiterated in the foreword to the Second *Penguin Book of English Stories*, published in 1972, in which Dolley writes (about the multi-language companion editions): 'their pub-lication has demonstrated that, far from continuing its supposed decline, the short story is enjoying a revival' (1972, p.7). However, Hudson and Dolly's concerns were unfounded: the *Penguin Book of English Stories*, for example, has been reprinted frequently in the last, almost, fifty years (Prescott, 2016).[5]

Much previous scholarship centres upon the type of anthologies where poems, prose, and essays are removed from their original home and placed in a new one, often out of context (Gerson, 1989; Pace, 1992; Mujica, 1997). This type of anthology is often, as Germano (2001) suggests, 'unfairly regarded with some disdain, as if the anthology were in itself a middlebrow enterprise, crafted to eliminate the difficult or the provo-cative' (p.136). In fact, Epstein (2001) goes as far as to say, 'Anthologies serve no literary purpose, usually find few readers and quickly go out of print' (p.139–40). However, Price (2000) demonstrates how various lit-erary genres from the eighteenth and nineteenth centuries, such as the gothic and the epistolary novel, were significantly influenced by readers' desire to have their components featured in anthologies. This allowed

---

[5] The last reprinting was in 2011.

(some) readers to give the impression that they had read the full version of the book – and thus be considered as members of a high-status group – when they had, in fact, simply skimmed the excerpts in an anthology. Furthermore, Price contends that until the twentieth century, a noteworthy work of literature was essentially synonymous with being 'widely anthologized' (p. 70).

Canon [and Identity] Formation

Anthologies serve as a means of selecting and presenting a subset of literary works that are believed to be representative of a specific genre, period, culture, or theme (Price, 2000). The act of choosing which works to include and exclude helps shape the perception of what is considered culturally significant and worthy of reading and/or study (Gorak, 1991; Lauter, 1991; Guillory, 1993; Kaplan & Rose, 1996). While anthologies of new writing can bring previously unpublished stories, and sometimes authors, into the world, Prescott (2016) argues that 'the canon-forming function of anthologies is most clearly evident when there is a longer historical perspective on the selection' (p.565). Anthologies are often put together by editors, scholars, or institutions with certain perspectives, biases, and preferences. As gatekeepers of literature, these individuals or groups exert influence over which works are elevated to canonical status. This can impact the visibility and recognition of certain authors and works while excluding others. In fact, Kilcup (2000) argues that 'composing an anthology creates a miniature canon, no matter how resistant the editor is to vexed notions of goodness and importance' (p.37). As Hopkins (2008, p.287) argues, 'The processes of anthologising, canon-formation, and literary judgement, are intimately bound up one with another.' Over time, anthologies can change to reflect shifting cultural norms and expanding perspectives. March-Russell (2009) argues that literary anthologies have played a pivotal role in 'recording the impact [. . .] of historical movements such as modern feminism, Gay Liberation and post-colonialism' and thus occupied a central position in the initial cultural discussions concerning questions of identity and representation (p.58). This led to anthologies being part of the 'canon wars' that occurred in the US in the 1980s, as Price (2000) notes: 'the canon wars of the

1980s were fought over anthologies' tables of contents' (p.2). There was a tension during this period, Guillory (1993) argues, between perceived literary value and 'representing the consensus of some community, either dominant or subordinate' (p.29). It was during the 1970s and 1980s that a subset of anthology, focusing on identity-themed new writing by under-represented voices, began to emerge.[6] New editions of anthologies including underrepresented voices allow for a more expansive canon. This dynamic process can lead to the re-evaluation and expansion of what is considered canonical. Anthologies of new collections of writing can there-fore subvert this canon-forming process, or at least help construct new canons, which strengthen and promote a new generation of voices and cultural works. Srivastava (2010) mentions the dual role of anthologies, 'as much innovators as conservators of the canon and, in many cases, they offer to their readers writing that makes a decisive intervention in society and culture' (p.162). Social marginalisations – such as social class, race/ethnicity, gender identity, sexuality – find their meanings in particular historical contexts and locations. Anthologies during the twentieth century contribut-ed to the development of inclusion, diversity, and identity-formation, challenged the canon, and continue to this day.

Anthologies Today

Contemporary anthologies continue to reflect the evolving literary and cultural landscape. Digital technology has transformed the way anthologies are created and distributed. Online platforms allow for more immediate and

---

[6] For example *Cuentos: Stories by Latinas* (1983), *Girl Next Door: Lesbian Feminist Stories* (1985), and *Out Front: Contemporary Gay and Lesbian Plays* (1988), *Charting the Journey: Writings about Black and Third World Women* (1988). 'Underrepresented voices' here refers to socially marginalised groups, for example BIPOC and LGBTQIA+. There were, of course, earlier anthologies by women writers; Blain, Clements, and Grundy (1990) note evidence of such anthologies going back to the sixteenth century. Additionally, Chester (2022) provides a history of feminist anthologies, including those such as *The Body Politic: Women's Liberation in Britain 1969–1972* (1972), which proliferated in the UK in the 1970s.

widespread access, whilst the internet and social media have also enabled collaborative and crowdsourced anthologies, where a diverse range of voices can contribute and shape the content. These technological changes have helped to democratise the anthology process and challenges traditional notions of authority and expertise.

Anthologies that centred around new writing increased in popularity in the twenty-first century. In the UK, some of these were linked to literary prizes, such as the Bristol Short Story Prize, while others are published on an annual basis, such as Salt Publishing's *Best British Short Stories* series (Prescott, 2016).[7] The importance of such anthologies cannot be overstated. Boyd Tonkin's review, of the 2013 edition, said, 'This [the Salt *Best British Short Stories* series] annual feast satisfies again. Time and again, in Royle's crafty editorial hands, closely observed normality yields (as Nikesh Shukla's spear-fisher grasps) to the things we "cannot control"' (Salt, 2023). The reason this review quotation was chosen, over many others, was because Nikesh Shukla – whose short story 'Canute' appeared in the 2013 edition – has played an important role in the rise of anthologies by BPOC authors in the UK since 2016. Shukla is now a prominent member of the UK literary scene and has acknowledged how inclusion in his first anthology, and the support of other BPOC authors, were 'responsible' for the launch of his career (see Chapter 3). He has written and published six books since this 2013 anthology. It is interesting to note that Shukla wrote and published several short stories before 'Canute' but has not been as prolific a short-story writer since his rise to literary prominence. We might infer, from this, that the short story is a form that is most beneficial to new and emerging authors; something that is explored in more depth in Chapter 3.

British Multicultural Anthologies

As Chapters 2 and 3 will demonstrate, there has been a spate of anthologies that look at different identities in recent years: in particular, multi-genre anthologies by marginalised people are on the rise. This is counter to some of the more traditional anthologies whose focus on traditional aesthetics, including genre,

---

[7] The annual anthology is now in its fourteenth year.

works against marginalised authors (Lauter, 2004). Collections of short stories by BPOC British authors, or even the inclusion of BPOC authors in anthologies, have been scarce. For example, the *Oxford Book of English Short Stories*, edited by A.S. Byatt, does not feature any BPOC British authors (Prescott, 2016).

Formerly independent, Birmingham-based publisher Tindal Street Press was responsible for publishing some influential anthologies in the 2000s, publishing new voices alongside established authors.[8] *Whispers in the Walls* (2001), edited by Leone Ross and Yvonne Brissett, for example, concentrated on new Black and Asian voices from Birmingham in a time where these voices – Black, Asian, and regional – were a particular rarity in publishing. Projects such as this, and the subsequent anthologies (by Tindal Street) like *Mango Shake* (2006) edited by Debjani Chatterjee and *Too Asian, Not Asian Enough* (2011) edited by Kavita Bhanot, bring attention to less-well-known, regional, authors and differently positioned subjectivities in addition to allowing diasporic self-representation, beyond the exoticising gaze of imagined mainstream audiences. For example, *Too Asian, Not Asian Enough* is a precursor to many of the subsequent British anthologies, such as *A Change Is Gonna Come*, which look at experiences beyond the stereotypes. As the editor Kavita Bhanot (2011a), mentions in the foreword:

> Born or brought up in Britain, we suffer at the hands of oppressive parents. These comical or villainous figures hold us back from the pleasures of Western life: they don't let us drink alcohol or eat meat; they force us to wear suits or keep top-knots. They want us to have arranged marriages. When we resist, they resort to emotional blackmail or physical force. (p.i)

Bhanot (2011a) argues that this has 'become a cliché dominating British Asian narratives. It has become "a bankable, marketable formula" (p.ix), and it is stifling to a new generation of writers who don't want to conform to its

[8] Tindal Street Press was bought by independent publisher Profile Books in 2012 and is now based at their London offices.

conventions'. Saha and van Lente (2022) describe the paradoxical nature of this racialising logic, which positions BIPOC authors using these clichéd themed and problem-based narratives, that Bhanot outlines, to sell more books. However, not only do these stereotypical narratives stifle new authors, as Bhanot states, but it also pushes these titles out of the mainstream and into niche interest categories (Saha & van Lente, 2022).

Bhanot (2011b) describes the duality BPOC British authors face,

> The diversity of the stories in this anthology highlights how problematic and forced categories can be, which expect writers to write a certain kind of story, depending on their surname, religion, skin colour. On the other hand, I do think that there is something that we share, in terms of our histories of colonialism, as immigrants or descendants of immigrants, because of our skin colour.

Bhanot (2011b) noted that contributors to the anthology 'seemed to relish the freedom the anthology gave them'. Consequently, the stories within this anthology cover a wide range of topics, set in different parts of the world, such as a cocaine-fuelled party in London (Nikesh Shukla/'Iron Nose') and hair collecting in a European village (Niven Govinden/'La Coiffeuse'). Anthologies play a crucial role in shaping and strengthening communities for underrepresented authors: this will be explored further in Chapter 3. Through these Tindal Street anthologies, we begin to see a community of BPOC British authors forming, with each new anthology adding new authors into the community.[9] The collaborative nature of multi-authored books, such as anthologies, reflects a collective commitment to change. Collaborating on a multi-authored anthology can foster a sense of community among the authors and their readers. By working together towards a common goal, authors build solidarity, mutual support, and collective resilience. This sense of community can extend beyond the pages of the

---

[9] Since being bought by, and becoming an imprint of, independent publisher Profile Books in 2012, Tindal Street has not published any further anthologies by BPOC British writers.

book, as we will see in the discussion about crowdfunding, inspiring readers to become more actively involved in activist efforts and grassroots movements. Nikesh Shukla, as noted earlier, began contributing to such anthologies and, in recent years, has made a major contribution to their resurgence, in the UK, through editing *The Good Immigrant* (2016).

The success of *The Good Immigrant* anthology, could be in part responsible for the rise in popularity of anthologies in the British publishing industry. *The Good Immigrant*, is a collection of twenty-one essays by BPOC British artists, comedians, writers, academics, professionals, and journalists, who speak about their experiences of being othered in their own country. The essays explore the examination of a British national culture and national identity entangled in a state of nostalgia linked to British imperialism. A prevalent theme running through these essays is how BPOC authors must emphasise their racial identities for the benefit of their (often predominantly white) readers because of the construction of a supposedly universal white experience. On the opposite side to this, demonstrating the impact of whiteness as a default on young people, Darren Chetty's 'You Can't Say That! Stories Have to Be about White People' highlights the serious issue of BPOC children not seeing themselves as the protagonists in stories. Numerous essays address the fallacies surrounding the concept of the Asian 'model minority' and the oversimplified portrayal of a monolithic Black identity. For example, in 'Beyond "Good" Immigrants', Wei Ming Kam surmises that 'being a model minority is code for being on perpetual probation' (p. 95). While Reni Eddo-Lodge, author of the bestselling *Why I'm No Longer Talking to White People About Race*, outlines,

> To be an immigrant, good or bad, is about straddling two homes, whilst knowing you don't really belong to either. It is about both consuming versions of blackness, digging around in history until you get confirmation that you were there, whilst creating your own for the present and the future. It is up to you to make your own version of blackness in any way you can – trying on all the different versions, altering them until they fit. (p.83)

The impact of *The Good Immigrant* has been widespread. Not only did its publication lead to the launch of *The Good Journal*, a crowdfunded literary magazine, but it also resulted in the establishment of The Good Literary Agency, a social enterprise literary agency that centres on authors from underrepresented groups. The influence also extended beyond the UK, when *The Good Immigrant USA* was published in 2019. Additionally, how *The Good Immigrant* came to be published highlighted a new reader-/audience-led publishing model, since it was a publication crowdfunded through Unbound (a UK-based crowdfunding publisher). Crowdfunding can provide important opportunities for BIPOC authors, who face systemic barriers in accessing traditional sources of funding for creative projects including publishing. Platforms and publishers such as Unbound provide an alternative avenue for raising capital without relying on traditional gate-keepers, who may have biases or limited understanding of BIPOC narratives and perspectives. Crowdfunding, therefore, allows BIPOC authors to maintain autonomy and creative control over their projects. Instead of conforming to the preferences or expectations of traditional publishers, creators can directly engage with their audience and produce works that authentically represent their experiences, cultures, and voices. Bond (2019) argues, therefore, that *The Good Immigrant* is an example of 'the anthologising impulse of this sort of collective, participatory action' (p.171). In fact, the anthology reached its crowdfunding target in three days, in part due to the visibility of donations from authors such as J.K. Rowling, David Nicholls, Jonathan Coe, and Evie Wyld (Lea, 2015). Crowdfunding can, therefore, turn passive reader-consumers into empowered investors in the arts (or 'fanvestors', as Galuszka & Bystrov (2014) describe them), who are largely motivated by the symbolic capital of being part of an 'early-adopter' community (Gehring & Wittkower, 2015).[10] Crowdfunding can also be a form of 'commodity activism' where consumers invest in commodities to participate in social justice movements (Mukherjee & Banet-Weiser, 2012).

---

[10] As Gehring & Wittkower (2015) argue, 'The cultural cachet of early adoption or insider access is well established outside of the crowdfunding model, as in the backstage pass or in having been a fan of something "before it was cool"' (p.68).

As noted, *The Good Immigrant* came at an important time in the 'diversity' conversation in the United Kingdom, when authors (including Shukla) were tiring of diversity initiatives and panels that brought about no discernible change. It was also published in a tumultuous period in the UK, during the United Kingdom European Union membership referendum, where questions about national identity and Britishness were at the fore. The culture wars – the tensions between conservative and progressive – worldviews came to a head during this period, and British society has become increasingly divided since. Immigrants and 'race'/ethnicity more generally have been central to the culture wars (Duffy et al., 2021). Like other contemporary anthologies, *The Good Immigrant* attempts to revise and reshape national identity; this is reminiscent of anthologies, and some of the tensions, in the past. According to both Price (2000) and Benedict (2015), early anthologies attempted to create a national literary identity. In the US, the proliferation of anthologies in the nineteenth century was a reaction to the overarching belief that there was no American Literature since the market over-relied on imports from the UK (Gailey, 2020). While, as noted earlier, scholars have made the link between the 'canon wars' in the 1980s and 1990s, and the rise in more representative and expansive anthologies (Guillory, 1993; Bona, 2017).

The publication of *The Good Immigrant*, and its predecessors, have given rise to a wealth of British anthologies by BPOC authors, focusing on different ethnicities, genres, and topics. These include *The Things I Would Tell You: British Muslim Women Write* (2017), *Voices of the Windrush Generation: The Real Story Told by the People Themselves* (2020), *Cut from the Same Cloth?: Muslim Women on Life in Britain* (2021), *Black British Lives Matter* (2022), and *East Side Voices: Essays Celebrating East and Southeast Asian Identity in Britain* (2022). In recent years, there has been a noticeable rise in the publication of YA anthologies, particularly by authors whose work and or identities fall outside the boundaries of the mainstream (Jensen, 2020; Grochowski, 2021). YA fiction offers a rich and dynamic case study for exploring issues of exclusion due to its wide-ranging target audience (from adolescents to adult readers), growing emphasis on authenticity and representation, exploration of social issues, and evolution as a field of literature. Drawing upon the histories outlined in Chapter 1, the rising trend for YA anthologies is examined and analysed in greater detail in Chapter 2.

2 The Development of YA Anthologies

The YA market in the UK, and beyond, has grown exponentially since the publication, and subsequent blockbuster film adaptations, of what Fitzsimmons and Wilson call the 'YA hypercanon' (Fitzsimmons & Wilson, 2020; Ramdarshan Bold, 2021). These books, which typically centre on dominant group characters (e.g. white, heterosexual, cisgender, and non-disabled protagonists) and are written by authors who share these demographics, catapulted YA into the mainstream public's consciousness. Despite this growth and the resounding popularity of YA, there is a dearth of 'diverse' YA authors (i.e. those from socially marginalised communities). In fact, only one of the bestselling UK YA titles of 2006–2016 was written by a 'diverse' British author (Malorie Blackman) while 90 per cent of titles featured white, heterosexual, non-disabled, cisgender protagonists (human or otherwise) (Ramdarshan Bold, 2018). The marginalisation of minoritised authors and characters has a long history, which has engendered a cultural hierarchy in publishing output (Ramdarshan Bold, 2019a, 2021; Sands-O'Connor, 2023). This imbalance affects aspiring and emerging authors who are trying to break into the market as well as established midlist authors, who, despite being undervalued, prop up an industry focused on bestsellers (Ramdarshan Bold, 2019b). YA anthologies – such as those detailed later in this chapter – are making a direct intervention in the publishing industry by featuring authors from socially marginalised groups, increasing representation, and taking full advantage of the short story's capacity to depict marginalised experiences. More recent anthologies are centring protagonists with varying intersectional identities. These types of texts, according to Gopinath (2018, p.16), 'do things in the world: they shift our vision so that alternative possibilities, landscapes, and geographies come into view'. This chapter looks at how YA anthologies have developed over the decades, using some example texts to illustrate how these have changed alongside changes in society and the way young people read/ young people's interests.

As noted earlier, anthologies can be collections of work (previously or newly published) by various authors or by one author: YA antholo-gies typically fall into the first category of authorship. Most examples of single-authored YA anthologies are by prominent authors writing in the science-fiction and/or fantasy genre. For example, Veronica Roth, author of the *Divergent* series, wrote *The End and Other Beginnings: Stories from the Future*, a collection of six short stories published in 2019. These novella-length stories all have a science-fiction element like Roth's previous work; two of the stories are situated in the *Carve the Mark* universe. *The Poison Eaters and Other Stories* (2010) is Holly Black's, author of *The Spiderwick Chronicles* amongst other books, single-authored collection of (some previously published) fantasy short stories.[11] Like Roth, Black revisits some of her previous paranormal worlds – such as the *Modern Faerie Tale* series – and characters in this collection. Black has also edited several, multi-authored YA anthologies: *Geektastic: Tales from the Nerd Herd* (2009),[12] *Zombies Vs. Unicorns* (2010), and *Welcome to Bordertown* (2011). Like other fields and genres, single-authored YA anthologies are the domain of writers, usually novelists, with established reputations (Prescott, 2016). Towards the latter half of the 2010s, YA anthologies began to focus more on socially marginalised authors, possibly due to the growing community of authors, and readers, calling for more inclusive books.

The Rise of Inclusive YA Anthologies

YA anthologies have been in existence for decades. Like most trends, however, their popularity has fluctuated, with a resurgence over the last few years. Since the early 2000s, there was a proliferation of YA anthologies – collections of short stories – that centred around a single topic. The bulk of these collections feature short fictional stories around a particular theme, ranging from prom dates to beauty, from friendships to geekiness, and from LGBTQIA+ stories to stories that targeted specifically gendered readers. Unlike anthologies of the past, recent YA anthologies do not consecrate or canonise YA authors. Some,

---

[11] Some of the short stories were previously published in *21 Proms*, *The Faery Reel*, and *The Restless Dead* anthologies.

[12] *Geektastic*, as noted earlier, brought together some bestselling YA authors – such as Cassandra Clare, Cynthia Leitich Smith, John Green, and David Levithan – to celebrate geekiness in all its forms.

like *A Change Is Gonna Come*, have demonstrated the unequal conditions of literary production that perpetuates the current literary system. While others, like the ones highlighted later in this chapter, celebrate a diverse range of authors and writing across a multitude of topics and genres. There has been a clear growth in the presence of protagonists and authors from socially marginalised groups in/writing YA over the last decade (Ramdarshan Bold, 2021). These stories have, particularly in the last few years, began to evolve from 'issue books' to more complex and nuanced stories in a variety of forms and genres, for example, *The Poet X* by Elizabeth Acevedo, the *Heartstopper* series by Alice Oseman, *Pet* by Akwaeke Emezi, *Laura Dean Keeps Breaking Up with Me* by Mariko Tamaki, *The Black Flamingo* by Dean Atta, *Cinderella Is Dead* by Kalynn Bayron, *Hani and Ishu's Guide to Fake Dating* by Adiba Jaigirdar, *And the Stars Were Burning Brightly* by Danielle Jawando, and *Some Like It Cold* by Elle McNicoll (to name a few). This expansion means that we are also beginning to see more hybrid and intersectional identities, with a much wider spectrum of characters. The examples and very brief histories detailed in the rest of this chapter are simply a snapshot to illustrate the broader concepts and trends under discussion in this Element.

Queer Anthologies

Many anthologies have a particular angle or focus, such as sexuality and sexual identity. These emerging LGBTQIA+ narratives are counter to earlier depictions of queer people in books and the media, where most queer characters were secondary and used to forward the journey of the heterosexual protagonist. As Banks (2009) outlines:

> Most of the LGBT characters in YA fiction were secondary, often dead or killed off during the narrative, or run out of town and separated from community and/or family. The message is hard to miss: LGBT characters are most useful if they're dead and gone. (p.35)

Although depictions began to proliferate in the 1970s and 1980s, with a growing number of queer protagonists, Jenkins (1998) found that these characters fell into a very narrow demographic and that stereotypical stories abounded: 'the majority of the titles reinforced social stereotypes of the generic gay person as an urban middle-class white male who is educated, involved in the arts, and likely to encounter hardships directly related to antigay prejudice' (p.300). Things began to improve in the 1990s, with inclusion of a wider range of sexualities and gender identities being portrayed (Wickens, 2011). However, these depictions were often simplistic and, as we will shortly in this chapter, still fell under the realm of the problem novel (Banks, 2009). Most of these anthologies, particularly those published in the twentieth and early twenty-first centuries, were published in the US and featured US authors. In the UK, Section 28 – a 12- to 15-year-old piece of legislation enacted by the Conservative government in 1988 – prohibited the promotion of homosexuality in schools and local authorities, effectively censoring discussion and representation of LGBTQIA+ topics in education and public institutions (Simpson, 2020). Consequently, Section 28 impacted the types of books published for children and young people in the UK and, relevant to this chapter, inhibited the growth of Queer UKYA until the legislation was repealed in 2000 (in Scotland) and 2003 (in England and Wales) (Simpson, 2021).

Jensen (2020) identifies *Am I Blue? Coming Out From The Silence*, edited by Marion Dane Bauer and published in 1995, as one of the earliest YA anthologies. This anthology, which features well-known US authors such as Jacqueline Woodson, Francesca Lia Block, and Lesléa Newman, centres on the experiences of gay and lesbian teenagers or those with gay or lesbian parents. *Queer 13*, edited by Clifford Chase, followed shortly afterwards in 1998. This collection of autobiographical essays details the contributors' – including Jacqueline Woodson, David Bergman, and Rebecca Walker – experiences of being lesbian and gay thirteen-year-olds. Such anthologies coincided with, in the US, the public's changing attitudes towards the lesbian and gay community, instigated by the nation's youth, and an increase in the number of lesbian and gay television characters (Seidman, 2002; Savin-Williams, 2005; Garretson, 2018). It was during the 1990s that coming out as a concept and process created a new publishing phenomenon: self-help books to help guide and advise people in the LGBTQIA+ community, and also their family, friends, co-workers, educators, and so on, through the coming out process (Johnson, 1997; Savin-Williams, 2001; Sullivan, 2003).

Many of the stories in the two aforementioned anthologies focus on the coming out narrative, a type of story that emerged in the 1970s that has been prevalent in literature, film, and other media since (Cart & Jenkins, 2006; Saxey, 2008; Bobker, 2015; Abate, 2017). Dane Bauer, outlines in her introduction of *Am I Blue? Coming Out from The Silence*, that 'One out of ten teenagers attempts suicide [. . .] One out of three of those does so because of concern about being homosexual' (1995, p.2), so reading an anthology of coming out stories can be comforting and empowering for young queer readers. However, coming out narratives can also be othering, and dictated by heterosexuality, as Barker argues, '[p]eople wouldn't have to come out if heterosexuality wasn't the assumed norm' (Barker, 2016, p.92). Roof (1996) describes coming out stories as 'folktales', considering them as formulaic and serving a particular social purpose. She argues that for lesbian characters, this type of plot can be very restrictive: 'Why is the story always the same? [. . .] While for lesbian cultures the coming out story might be liberating, in a more inclusive cultural picture it limits the potential roles and functions of lesbian characters' (Roof, 1996, p.xxvi). According to Cart and Jenkins(2006), the earliest LGBTQIA+ (at the time, typically gay and lesbian) YA books were usually issue books/problem novels, that centred on 'a character who has not previously been considered gay/lesbian comes out either voluntarily or involuntarily' (p.xiv). This established homosexuality as something negative that it was 'dangerous to be queer, one is punished for being queer, queer relationships are bound to end badly, being queer is just a phase, and so forth' (Cart & Kaywell, 2018, p.2). Both anthologies were written close to thirty years ago, so some of the topics and tropes in the stories are outdated and problematic (Cart & Jenkins, 2006). For example, the representation of different sexualities is limited, there is biphobia in some of the stories (e.g. in 'Am I Blue'/Bruce Coville), and, as noted, many of the stories contain outdated tropes (e.g. the 'Bury Your Gays' trope in 'Hands'/Jonathan London, the gay teacher dies from AIDS). There are also violent incidents of homophobia is several of the stories (e.g. the main character Vince in 'Am I Blue'/Bruce Coville is 'gaybashed' by the school bully); these, as Crisp (2009) writes, 'use homophobia as the foil against which characters with non-normative sexual identities struggle in order to find happiness' (p.335–336). This, again, links Queer YA to the sphere of problem novels where the protagonist's sexuality is an 'issue'. While homophobia, and bullying and violence related to homophobia, are something that many young queer people experience, Banks (2009) summarises why these one-dimensional representations can be damaging, 'While these conflicts may be "realistic," they are also reductive when rendered as a canon of available literature, suggesting that the experiences of being queer are only about these personal conflicts, not about larger issues or more complex experiences with the world' (p.35). Scholars of YA have since written about the impact of such negative tropes on contemporary YA, despite there being more Queer YA – showcasing a broader spectrum of queer identities – now than ever before (see, for example: Kidd, 1998; Banks, 2009; Crisp, 2009; Cart & Kaywell, 2018; Duckels, 2021; Henderson, 2021; Mason, 2021; Matos, 2021; Simpson, 2021).

As the field of YA grew and developed in the 2000s, so did the number of anthologies. It was during the first decade of the 2000s that Queer YA had 'begun to move – as have many of the individual titles that comprise it – toward assimilation; moving, that is, from being an isolated or "ghettoized" subgenre to becoming a more integrated part of the total body of young adult literature' (Cart & Jenkins, 2006, p.128). This was also happening alongside the rise in popularity of television programmes that centred on gay, typically white, men such as *Will and Grace* and *Queer Eye for the Straight Guy*. Although these programmes were very popular and watched widely – *Will and Grace* had a larger viewing audience than *The Simpsons* at one point – Crisp (2009) argues that, 'Rather than "mainstream" acceptance of non-normative sexual identities, these representations of gay characters are frequently molded to fit into a heteronormative frame' (p.334). This, alongside some of the issues from earlier Queer YA anthologies, was present in YA anthologies published during this period. David Levithan played an important role in the development of Queer YA, in his groundbreaking book *Boy Meets Boy*, which, Crisp argues, 'constructs a world of possibilities beyond heteronormativity' (2009, p.340). Levithan also spearheaded numerous Queer YA anthologies during this period, such as editing *The Full Spectrum: A New Generation of Writing about Gay, Lesbian, Bisexual,*

Transgender, Questioning, and Other Identities (2006). While this multi-genre anthology – showcasing essays, journal entries, poems, and photographs – purports to explore different identities within the LGBTQIA+ community, it focuses predominantly on gay, lesbian, and transgender stories. Like other Queer YA at the time, many of the stories 'rely upon homophobia and homophobic discourse to provide readers with a sense of "realism"' (Crisp, 2009, p.339). However, this, and other anthologies edited by Levithan, showcase the creativity of young people: this particular anthology includes writing by forty young people (under 24) from the LGBTQIA+ community. In collaboration with PUSH Scholastic, Levithan also published three anthologies (2002, 2005, 2008) showcasing YA authors within the imprint.

Although some of the earlier Queer YA anthologies included BIPOC authors and thus showcased a broader queer experience, many of the stories were very US-centric. While this (US focus) is still, for the most part, the case, more recent Queer YA anthologies include more varieties of sexuality and gender identities. Three anthologies, edited by US author Saundra Mitchell, were published in quick succession as a companion trilogy of sorts: *All Out: The No-Longer-Secret Stories of Queer Teens throughout the Ages* (2018); *Out Now: Queer We Go Again!* (2020); and *Out There: Into the Queer New Yonder* (2022). *All Out* puts queer people in different periods throughout history – from 1300s England ('Every Shade of Red'/Elliot Wake; a transgender Robin Hood retelling) to the most recent turn of the millennium in Boston, US ('The End of the World as We Know It'/Sara Farizan; set during New Year's Eve with Y2K panic looming). While trying to represent the wider spectrum of sexualities, the anthology mostly centres on cis-gendered, LGB characters. The anthology does, however, include a story – 'And They Don't Kiss at the End' by Nilah Magruder – about a Black teenager understanding her asexuality, in the 1970s, when she does not have the language to describe how she is feeling. However, Dee, the protagonist, does accept her identity in the end saying, 'I like what I like and I don't like what I don't. I have nothing to apologize for.' The importance of this anthology is the representation of queer people in historical fiction. Bravmann (1997) argues that historical narratives have a powerful social, cultural, and political role in helping queer people construct their identities and creating collective and individual meaning. Although queer people have been in existence throughout history, LGBTQIA+ history is often hidden, constrained, or erased due to repressive social attitudes and criminal persecution. For example, despite discriminatory legislation such as the 'Don't Ask, Don't Tell' (DADT) in the US, transgender people (in addition to other people from the LGBTQIA+ community), as Whitt (2022) argues, 'have *always* served in military organizations' (p.15).[13] Brown (1988) found that transgender solders enlisted in the military for numerous reasons, including unhappy homelives and as a way of 'purging their cross-gender identifications' (p. 535). This type of history is written about in 'Roja' by Anna-Marie McLemore, one of the stories in *All Out*. Set in nineteenth-century Mexico, the protagonist's love interest, León, is a trans soldier and prison of war. Aligning with Brown's (1988) findings, León is not openly trans to his fellow soldiers:

> 'No one, not *la Légion*, not Oropeza, ever knew León as anything but a boy. They did not know that his mother had christened him with a girl's name. They did not know that he had joined *la Légion* less out of patriotism and more for the chance to live as who he was' (para. 66). However, to Emilia, his love interest, he is simply León, 'I called him by his true name, León, the one he'd chosen himself. None of this was strange to me, a boy choosing his own name' (para. 3).

The follow-on anthology, *Out Now: Queer We Go Again*, has more of a contemporary focus, with some speculative fiction, and a wider representation of ethnicities, sexualities, and body types. While it also features mostly LGB characters there are more non-binary, asexual, and demi-sexual

---

[13] DADT was a US policy regarding military service by lesbian, gay, and bisexual (LGB) people. Introduced by President Bill Clinton's administration in 1993, the policy basically mandated that military personnel do not ask about a service member's sexual orientation and that service members do not reveal their sexual orientation. Before this policy, Article 125 of the Uniform Code of Military Justice effectively barred gay people from openly serving in the US military (Nicholson, 2012).

characters than its predecessor. The anthology also includes contributions by two trans authors – Meredith Russo ('The Coronation') and Fox Benwell ('Once Upon a Seastorm') – whose stories feature trans characters. Intersectionality is more of a theme in this second instalment, for example 'Floating'/Tanya Boteju is a romance story about a neurodivergent teenager. In comparison, *All Out, Out Now* also includes stories that may be relatable to teenagers today; for example, Mark Oshiro's 'Refresh' explores how we represent ourselves in photographs online, especially in the context of dating and romance. The conclusion to the trilogy *Out There: Into the Queer New Yonder* centres on speculative fiction narratives: all the stories are set in the future. Additionally, there is a wider spectrum of identities, and intersectional identities, in this final collection in comparison to the first two, for example more BIPOC, trans, non-binary, asexual, and demi-sexual characters. For example, 'Nick and Bodhi'/Naomi Kanakia features an Indian trans woman as the main character and 'Fractal Eyes'/Ugochi M. Agoawike features a Black non-binary protagonist. The combination of the different identities, the genres, and the diversity of the authorship (which is discussed in more depth later in this chapter) showcases how Queer YA anthologies have evolved over the years.

There have also been numerous other Queer YA anthologies published in recent years – and more general YA anthologies that feature queer characters, some explored later in this chapter – which have contributed to the development of the genre. Most of these, including the aforementioned anthologies, have a North American (mostly US) focus. In the UK, which has a different history with queer books for children and young people because of Section 28, the most prominent Queer YA anthology is *Proud* (2019) edited by Juno Dawson. Dawson establishes the mood to the anthology, in her foreword, when she outlines the political backdrop in which many queer people in the UK have grown up. Section 28 of the Local Government Act 1988 stated that local authorities (thus including schools and libraries): 'shall not intentionally promote homosexuality [. . .] or promote the teaching in any maintained school of the acceptability of homosexuality as a pretended family relationship' (legislation.gov.uk, 1988). *Proud* brings together a predominantly British cast of authors and illustrators and most of the stories are set in the UK and Ireland, so the anthology really adds to the growing body of British Queer YA stories.

Race and Ethnicity

The historical marginalisation of BIPOC authors and characters has perpetuated a racialised cultural hierarchy within the US and UK publishing
industries (Ramdarshan Bold, 2019a). This issue is also prevalent in YA
books and authorship. For example, despite many initiatives, conversations,
and conference panels, BPOC British YA (UKYA) authors are still not
visible in the bestseller charts, prominent books festivals, and prestigious
literary prizes (Ramdarshan Bold, 2021). This cultural imbalance affects
aspiring and emerging authors, trying to break into the market; however, it
also impacts established midlist authors, who, despite being undervalued,
prop up an industry that is focused on bestsellers. Chapter 3 explores this
issue in more depth – through a case study of a UKYA anthology –
however, this chapter highlights some of the prominent multicultural YA
anthologies that have been published in recent years. Many of these, as will
be explored later in this chapter, introduce, or expand upon, important
concepts and issues for the young, and not-so-young, reader.

Issues of racism, discrimination, and prejudice feature in many of the YA
Anthologies written by BIPOC authors, as they do in YA books (by
BIPOC authors) in general.[14] This is unsurprising, given the growing
white supremacy movement and its return to mainstream politics (Wilson,
2020). In the 'Global North', there has been a rise in Xenophobia and anti-
Immigrant sentiment in recent years (Kopyciok & Silver, 2021). In the
UK, post-the 2016 EU referendum and Brexit, hate crimes – including
harassment, assault, and violence – have increased significantly, with the
negative rhetoric being amplified by the British Conservative government's hostile immigration policies, including a 'Draconian' new 'Illegal
Migration Bill' (Taylor, 2023; Williams et al., 2023). Elsewhere in Europe,
the growing animosity towards immigrants and immigration has led to
the far right gaining prominence in local and national governments.
For example, Giorgia Meloni, a far-right, Populist politician, became
Italy's Prime Minister in 2022, using an anti-immigration stance to mobi-
lise support, while some Scandinavian countries, such as Denmark and

---

[14] Like queer narratives, stories with BIPOC characters were confined to the
    problem novel category in the past (Cart, 2016; Ramdarshan Bold, 2019a).

Sweden, have seen a rise in Islamophobia (also prevalent in countries such as France and Poland) and have been changing their immigration policies to make their countries less attractive to migrants (Bailey-Morley & Kumar, 2022; Mourlane, 2023). In the US, Donald Trump's presidency helped to mainstream far and extreme right – repacked as 'alt-right' – politics. Central to Trump's and, more broadly, the Republican's anti-immigrant rhetoric was the idea that immigrants crossing the (Southern) border pose a threat to the safety of US citizens (Finley & Esposito, 2020). Trump famously launched his presidential campaign by highlighting – in numerous 'explicitly xenophobic, anti-immigrant, racist' rants – the perceived dangers posed by Mexican immigrants to the US (Verea, 2018). It is unsurprising, therefore, that the immigrant experience is one that is often explored in books for adults and young people (Bond, 2019; Preston, 2019). However, these stories have not always been told from an authentic perspective, as can be seen from the backlash surrounding *American Dirt* by Jeanine Cummins (a white, US author). While this is an example from adult fiction, rather than YA, it typifies how racialised stereotypes still uphold white supremacy both intra- and extra-textually.[15] *American Dirt* is about a Mexican bookseller who must flee Mexico after her family is murdered by a drugs cartel; she ends up as an 'illegal' immigrant in the US. Since its publication it has received much criticism for being racist, xenophobic, and for perpetuating negative stereotypes about Mexican people, with critics calling it 'trauma porn' (Grady, 2020; Sánchez Prado, 2021; Shapiro, 2021). Sánchez Prado (2021) argues that, apart from 'the misrepresentation and commodification of Mexico in the

---

[15] There have also been numerous controversies in YA regarding authors from dominant groups writing outside of their lived experiences to create stereotypical narratives featuring protagonists from socially marginalised groups. A high-profile example of this was the backlash against Keira Drake's *The Continent* for its racist depictions of Indigenous people and for using a 'white saviour' narrative. These collective criticisms, of the advanced reader copy, resulted in the publisher delaying the publication date and Drake rewriting the book, employing four sensitivity readers, before publishing the revised version in 2018 (Drake, 2019).

book's form and construction', one of the issues was the publishers' 'aim to capitalize on a growing Latinx market and on the political visibility of the questions of immigration [. . .] while keeping the mainstream white audience constituting the publisher's core customer base' (p.372).[16] Books like *American Dirt*, Sánchez Prado surmises, that look at the experience of immigration through a white gaze are:

> not only cannibalizations of the stories of the Latinx and Latin American communities for the enjoyment of a majority-wide readership. They also enable the attempts at encroachment of the growing cultural markets appealing to these communities at the expense of Latinx cultural producers and sociopolitical priorities. (p.378)

It is, therefore, critical to counter these tokenistic, stereotypical, and inauthentic depictions with a wider range of stories and perspectives that give a more nuanced and complex understanding of the different immigration experiences.

Come On In: 15 Stories about Immigration and Finding Home (2021), edited by Adi Alsaid, tackles the emotional complexities of immigration from a variety of perspectives. The stories are all written by authors who are immigrants or the children of immigrants and showcases far-reaching immigration experiences, although most of these stories are about immigration to the US. As it says at the start of the book, 'The immigrant story is not one story. It is a collection' (p.ii). The stories do not shy away from some of the more brutal elements of migration: in 'The Curandera and the Alchemist'/Maria E. Andreu, we see the fear that law enforcement related to immigration – in this case, U.S. Immigration and Customs Enforcement (ICE) – can instil and how they can tear families apart; in 'The Trip'/Sona

---

[16] A note on terminology: this Element will use 'Latine' – a term used by young social activists in Spanish-speaking South and Central America (Schmidt, 2019) – because it 'embodies [. . .] inclusivity – across socioeconomic status, citizenship, education, gender identity, age groups and nations, while honoring the Spanish language in the process' (Ochoa, 2022). However, 'Latinx' will be used if the term is in direct quotes or book titles.

Charaipotra we see the humiliation people feel when they are detained and treated as criminals – in this case, like terrorists – because of the colour of their skin; and the painfulness of saying goodbye to loved ones, as Nafiza Azad notes in her story, 'All the Colors of Goodbye':

> I have been haphazardly saying goodbye to everything-even to the stones in the backyards-but only at this moment do I realize the immensity of goodbye. Only at this moment do I realize the brutality of it. What is goodbye? Does it mean I will see you again? Or perhaps I love you? Or perhaps it means hold on to me and don't let me go, because I am not certain I will be myself anywhere but here. (pp.19–20)

However, not all the anthologies are based on painful experiences of displacement but give wider perspectives on being on being young and BIPOC in the world today. *Color Outside the Lines* (2019), edited by Sangu Mandanna, is a multi-genre anthology that focuses on different types of interracial relationships and the challenges associated with them. The stories in the anthology are situated around the world – from Mexico to India to the US – and do not solely focus on romance, in fact there are several different genres in this anthology including science fiction, fantasy, and historical fiction. Themes within the book vary too: while racism is not the core component of the stories, discrimination and bigotry do, unsurprisingly, come up as themes. For example, 'Your Life Matters'/L.L. McKinney, which is a superhero narrative set during the Black Lives Matter movement, inverts the side-kick trope by having a Black, superhero protagonist with her white, side-kick of a girlfriend, whilst also exploring police brutality and anti-Black racism. While 'Sandwiched in Between' by Eric Smith brings up the problem with colour-evasiveness and unconscious prejudices, with Michael, the protagonist telling his Brown-skinned girlfriend Amina, 'We don't even see color in my family, you know?' (p.222). In 'Something Gay and Magical', Adam Silvera takes the opportunity to explicitly provide commentary about the importance of joyful LGBTQIA+ representation in books, whilst also referring to the problem with 'issue' books:

> Oliver is left only with 'contemporary realistic' or 'issues'
> novels – as if it's impossible to imagine what coming out and
> first crushes are like otherwise. He wants other worlds, too.
> He wants stories he hasn't lived, stories like the ones every-
> one else has read so often they don't even appreciate an
> invented world for the miracle that it is. (p.247)

Oliver's, the protagonist, interaction with Winter, his dark-brown-skinned love interest, also leads him to question his own white privilege:

> Embarrassment consumes him as quickly as his love of the
> book cover. In all his rage about never seeing enough gay
> heroes in books, he completely overlooked how he could
> always see white or white-passing people in TV shows and
> movies and pretty much any book cover. If Oliver wanted to
> dress up as Harry Potter or Luke Skywalker at some con-
> vention no one would bat an eye, whereas Winter would
> probably turn heads as the Hispanic Captain America or the
> brown Jon Snow. (p.249)

We Need Diverse Books (WNDB) have also released anthologies, in response to their movement, and in celebration of multicultural YA and authors. In the same vein as *Change* book, the case study in Chapter 3, these anthologies were run as competitions and include both established and emerging authors. So far, there have been five WNDB-affiliated antholo- gies: three aimed at a middle-grade audience and two aimed at a YA audience. Their first YA anthology, *Fresh Ink* (2018) edited by Lamar Giles, brings together some prominent USYA authors such as Jason Reynolds, Nicola Yoon, and Malinda Lo. In the introduction, the editor, Lamar Giles, outlines his own experience of growing to dislike books, despite being a voracious reader, due to the lack of Black characters in books.

It became pretty freaking clear that, book after book, adventure after adventure, the heroes weren't like me at all [. . .] I mean black boys. More often than not, if I ran across a character who shared my race and gender in a book he was a gross stereotype, comic relief, token sidekick, or, depending on genre (I'm looking at you, science fiction, fantasy, and horror), there to die so the real hero could fight another day. (p.1)

The anthology was born out of a desire to change these narratives and includes work by a range of BIPOC authors from different heritages and backgrounds.[17] It shies away from the problem novel genres that have been imposed on BIPOC authors for decades (Ramdarshan Bold, 2019a). While issues of racism do come up in the stories, they are not problem narratives; they are simply parts of the characters' lives, in the same way that it is part of most BIPOC's lives. For example, 'Don't Pass Me By'/Eric Gansworth, which follows Hubert an Indigenous American boy going to school outside of the Reservation, provides important commentary on how the North American school system treats Indigenous people and how whiteness is treated as the default. In one scene, a teacher provides two pencil colours – 'Flesh and Burnt Sienna' (p.50) – for an activity where the students must colour in an image of a boy and label the body parts. Hubert uses the Burnt Sienna – which was allocated for pubic and underarm hair – to colour in the skin and his black pen for the hair. In response, the following interaction occurs between Hubert and the teacher:

'I see. Hubert. But you know, the assignment wasn't a self-portrait.'
'It was, if you're white', I said. (p.52)

'One Voice: A Something In-Between Story'/Melissa de la Cruz is also about students, this time at university-level, being treated differently

---

[17] At the point of publication, there were still very few YA narratives by BIPOC authors.

because of the colour of their skin. For example, Yen-Yen (the main character) details the experience of walking alone, at night, as a woman of colour, 'I wouldn't have been thinking about anything except for my safety. I would have been tracking each of those blue emergency phones across the quad, calculating just how far I would have to run to reach one if someone were to attack me' (p.139).

Most of the stories are contemporary fiction – with romance at the core – but there are some elements of other genres including sci-fi and fantasy. Malinda Lo bridges these themes in 'Meet Cute', which sees Tamia, a Black girl dressed as Agent Scully (X-Files), and Nic, an Asian girl dressed as a gender-bent Lieutenant Hikaru Sulu (Star Trek), meeting and forming an attraction during a black-out at a Comic-con. During their time together the two girls talk about racism and sexism in geek culture – particularly how women of colour are treated. This type of sexism is introduced early in the story when a male attendee states, 'I hate it when girls think they can cosplay men [. . .] It always looks so lame' (p.15). In the US, where the story is set, geek culture is associated with white people and spaces such as comic conventions are mostly made up of white men (Jenkins, 2012; Flowers, 2018). Furthermore, the kinds of racism and sexism explored in 'Meet Cute' are prevalent in cosplaying, for example, Black cosplayers being told 'that character isn't Black' (Jenkins, 2020, p.158). As such, stories such as 'Meet Cute' are a powerful act of resistance to the whiteness of mainstream and geek culture alike. When people of colour cross racial boundaries through cosplay as white characters, they are challenging the literature and media that often marginalise them. This transformative act subverts the conventional portrayal of white (men and women) characters, highlighting the possibility that many of these characters could have been portrayed as people of colour. It serves as a revolutionary statement, reclaiming representation and visibility.

While the first WNDB anthology forefronts the voices of BIPOC authors, the second anthology looks at diversity more broadly focusing on gender identity, sexuality, 'race'/ethnicity, disability, and religion. *A Universe of Wishes: A We Need Diverse Books Anthology* (2021) edited by Dhonielle Clayton features fifteen short stories in the speculative fiction genre; a genre that, as will be discussed later in this chapter, is going through an overhaul in terms of representation and inclusion. As part of this, *A Universe of Wishes* includes stories set in both new and already established worlds. Folktales and fairytales, which are typically a part of a nation's cultural heritage, are reimagined through different perspectives. By reimagining these stories, the authors contribute to the promotion of a broader range of cultural narratives, ensuring that certain histories are not overlooked or lost over time and that the cultural richness and diversity within a nation are represented. (Haase, 2010). For example, 'Cristal Y Ceniza'/Anne-Marie McLemore is a queer reimagining of Cinderella, where the main character – a daughter with two mothers – travels to a neighbouring palace to appeal to the Royal Family to provide refuge for families affected by anti-same-sex-partnership rules in her homeland. In doing so, she attracts the attention of the Prince, who is trans; an accepted identity in his homeland:

> He laughed again. 'There is no one way for everyone like me. Some of us bind; some of us don't. Some wear one kind of clothing; some, all kinds'
>
> Envy fluttered through me. I couldn't imagine growing up in a kingdom where a single person would be allowed to wear a dress one day and trousers the next, where a boy like the one before me could let the shape of his chest show and still be acknowledged as the boy he was. (p.98)

Rapunzel is also reimagined in Zoraida Córdova's 'Longer than the Threads of Time'. Set in modern-day New York City, in the world of Córdova's *Brooklyn Brujas* series, the story follows Danaë, a girl who has been imprisoned in a magical tower in Central Park for decades. This is not the only story that uses familiar characters and/or worlds: 'A Royal Affair'/V.E. Schwab is set in the *A Darker Shade of Magic* universe and explores the romance between two of the characters, Rhy Maresh and Alucard Emery and 'The Scarlet Woman'/Libba Bray is set in the same work as the author's Gemma Doyle trilogy.

Many YA anthologies centre around a different ethnic group or geographic region. *Wild Tongues Can't Be Tamed: 15 Voices from the Latinx*

Diaspora (2021), edited by Saraciea J. Fennell is, according to the author Zoraida Córdova, a 'raw and unapologetic collection of essays and poetry that dismantle stereotypes about people from the Latin American diaspora' (Macmillan, 2023). Most of the authors in the collection are Afro-Latine /Black, and/or Indigenous; a group of people that are often ignored or erased from narratives Latine history and people (Flores, 2021). Anti-Blackness and colourism are themes covered by several of the essays in this anthology, as Fennell writes in her own essay, 'Half In, Half Out: Orbiting a World Full of People of Color': 'Everyone is conditioned to view Black people as if we don't matter. Even among the Black community, society finds ways to pit us against each other, from colorism to the critiquing of our hair, our bodies, and so forth' (para. 1). In 'Cuban Imposter Syndrome'/Zakiya N. Jamal, the author grapples with her own internalised anti-Blackness, and the stereotypes imposed on her, in addition to her experiences of being in a predominantly white Latine setting. Terminology, language, identities, and practices are interrogated in the essays and conversations about intersectionality are forefront. For example, as Janel Martinez addresses in 'Abuela's Greatest Gift':

> Not only does Latinidad erase Blackness and Indigenity, but it also relies on one's proximity to whiteness, as well as how much privilege one has based on gender, sexual preference, socioeconomic status, immigrant status, language spoken, and mobility, among other things. Those who find them-selves closest to what's 'socially acceptable' benefit most. (p.226)

This approach ensures that heterogeneous experiences are presented. A more recent anthology, *Magic Has No Borders* (2023), edited by Sona Charaipotra and Samira Ahmed, focuses on fantasy and science fiction stories by fourteen authors from the South Asian diaspora, showcasing the diversity of the region. The stories in the anthologies mix South Asian (mostly Hindu but some Muslim) mythology, folklore, and legends, with more contemporary YA topics such as queerness and the role of gender in society. 'Dismantle the Sun'/Sangu Mandanna, for example, includes numerous strong and determined young women characters, the main character Vira was a warrior, while 'Chudail'/Nikita Gill follows the relationship between the Chudail, a mythical, shape-shifting creature, and the enduring disappearances of girls. In the story, Nikita makes a clear statement about the Patriarchy and the gendering of blame, 'It was easier to blame a woman for what went wrong with the choices of men than it was for men to take responsibility for the harm they caused' (1:23:06). These stories help to dismantle stereotypes about South Asian girls and women, who have oftentimes, been positioned as submissive, as victims, and/or, as Lau (2003) argues, 'defined in relation to others and, most frequently, in relation to her men folk' (p.369).

The proliferation of Black Lives Matter as a global movement brought YA anthologies devoted to showcasing Black authors and stories to the fore. *Black Enough: Stories of Being Young & Black in America* (2019), edited by the Haitian American YA author Ibi Zoboi, displays the spectrum of Black identities in the US. The anthology brings together a prestigious group of best-selling, award-winning, and emerging African American YA authors – including YA superstars such as Nic Stone, Jason Reynolds, Renée Watson, and Justina Ireland – to create a wide variety of intersectional representation. The seventeen stories in this collection both subvert and solidify stereotypes of Black teenagers in the US. There are some elements, such as connection to hair, that establish a Black cultural identity within the texts; however, the intersection of identities of the characters – with a variety of ethnicities, sexualities, religions, and family structures – expands definitions of what it means to be Black. Zoboi outlines her aim for the book in the introduction:

> What are the cultural threads that connect Black people all over the world to Africa? How have we tried to maintain certain traditions as part of our identity? And as teenagers, do we even care? These are the questions I had in mind when inviting sixteen other Black authors to write about teens examining, rebelling against, embracing, or simply existing within their own idea of Blackness. (p.2)

In response, each author explores their character's relationship with their racial identity in very different ways. For example, in 'Kissing Sarah Smart'/Justina Ireland, a mixed heritage, bisexual teenager grapples with her sexuality during a summer romance with a local, white girl, while dealing with her mother's mental health issues. While in 'The Ingredients'/Jason Reynolds, Black boyhood is celebrated when a group of teenage boys happily discuss sandwiches after visiting their local pool. Zoboi outlines, in the introduction:

> Like my revolutionary ancestors who wanted Haiti to be
> a safe space for Africans all over the globe, my hope is that
> *Black Enough* will encourage all Black teens to be their free,
> uninhibited selves without the constraints of being Black,
> too Black, or not Black enough. They will simply be enough
> just as they are. (p.1)

The celebration of Black joy is seen in two books edited by Dhonielle Clayton and written by six bestselling and critically acclaimed Black women: *Blackout* (2019) and its follow-up *Whiteout* (2023).[18] These books modify the anthology format by collecting interconnected short stories, by different authors, to create whole novels. In *Blackout* there are distinct chapters/short stories, where the author is identified; however, in *Whiteout* each chapter centres on a couple and the author's identity is kept a secret. As the titles suggest, *Blackout* follows six teenagers as they fall in love during a power outage in New York, while *Whiteout* follows twelve teenagers in Atlanta as they help a friend with a romantic gesture and apology during a snowstorm. Each anthology features sexuality diversity, different types of love and at different stages, and a variety of romantic tropes from second-chance love ('The Long Walk'/Tiffany D. Jackson, in *Blackout*, 'Ava and Mason' in *Whiteout*), to opposites attract ('Seymour and Grace'/Nicola Yoon, in *Blackout*), to forced proximity ('Made to fit'/Ashley Woodfolk in *Blackout*), to childhood friends to romantic partners ('All the Great Love

---

[18] Dhonielle Clayton, Tiffany D. Jackson, Nic Stone, Angie Thomas, Ashley Woodfolk, and Nicola Yoon.

Stories . . . and Dust'/Dhonielle Clayton, in *Blackout*, 'Jordyn' and 'Kaz' in *Whiteout*). Drawing upon Chapman's (2017) work, Lu and Knight Steele detail that 'Historically, blackness has been treated as the antithesis of life, and certainly disassociated from joy' (p.830). The cultural and creative industries, including the book publishing industry, have played a critical role in commodifying Black pain and trauma (Sobande, 2021). *Blackout* and *Whiteout*, therefore, act as a form of resistance to a society built on racism, violence, and oppression, and the books and literature that capitalise on this. As Dhonielle Clayton surmises in her story, in *Blackout*, 'All The Great Love Stories . . . and Dust', 'Some stories are better told in the dark. Not just the scary ones where someone gets chased through the woods. Or the whodunits where a bunch of suspects are trapped in a house. But even love stories can glow when the lights go out' (p.39).

Bodies and Minds

White/Eurocentric beauty standards are usually unrealistic, harmful, create social hierarchies based on body size, skin colour, hair colour, and so on, and are one of the key reasons that people, usually girls and women, develop poor body images (Mady et al., 2023). However, girls and women who adhere to these unrealistic standards are the ones promoted most favourably in the media, culture, and in advertising. Visual media, such as film and television, are also aggressive reinforcers of these standards (Groesz et al., 2002). These representations are particularly damaging to adolescents: commercial and advertising pressures have, therefore, contributed to teenagers struggling with their body image and, in some cases, their mental health (Mental Health Foundation, 2019; House of Commons Health and Social Care Committee, 2022). This has been compounded by the proliferation of social media and the ubiquity of digitally altered photographs (Meier & Gray, 2014; Fardouly & Vartanian, 2016). YA plays an important role in the relationship young readers develop with their bodies (Averill, 2016; Byers, 2018). Averill (2016) argues, 'the representations of fat people in young adult literature become quite powerful, as they serve as part of the foundation for how young people learn to interpret who fat people get to be and how culture will treat them' (p.14). Averill identifies how the fat body in YA has typically been used as cautionary tales, symbols of failure or limitation. This supports an earlier study by Rabinowitz (2003), who argues, 'Fatness is used overwhelmingly to connote corruption of inner character, weakness, immaturity, and flaws that need to be fixed' (p.1). Even the fat-acceptance narratives that Averill examined were set within the 'cultural framework of fat hatred' (p.21).

Fatphobia, Strings (2019) argues, is a product of white supremacy and originated with the racialisation of women's bodies, specifically Black women's bodies, during the transatlantic slave trade and the emergence of 'race science'. These historical tropes, about Black women's bodies (e.g. the Fat mammy figure) – which were constructed by enslavers as a form of control – persist in the media today (Collins, 2005; Coleman, 2011). It was through these racial discourses of fatness, which denigrated Black women, that thinness (and whiteness) was constructed as the norm because the manufactured fear of fatness (and Blackness) 'served as the driver for the creation of slenderness as the proper form of embodiment for elite white Christian women' (Strings, 2019, p.212). The media plays a critical role in shaping, mirroring, and strengthening societal standards, perceptions, and convictions concerning body weight and for perpetuating fatphobia (Thompson et al., 2005).

In a follow-up study to Averill (2016), Byers (2018, p.159) examines four more hopeful narratives with fat protagonists, which she argues 'open up alternative avenues through which to imagine futures long denied them'.[19] These more positive narratives have been published alongside the body positive movement, which has been popularised through social media platforms such as Instagram (Cohen et al., 2019). The body positivity movement – which celebrates all bodies – was started in response to unrealistic beauty standards; a social construct that promoted young, white, thin, non-disabled people/bodies (Sastre, 2014; Cohen et al., 2019; Rodgers et al., 2020). Quantitative and qualitative studies have found that the body positive movement – particularly viewing body positive images – has a positive impact on psychological wellbeing (Cohen et al., 2019; Rogers et al., 2020).

---

[19] *My Big Fat Manifesto* (2008), *Food, Girls, and Other Things I Can't Have* (2011), *Dumplin'* (2015), and *Holding Up the Universe* (2016).

In reflection of this, there have been some body-positive YA anthologies published in recent years. *The (Other) F Word: A Celebration of the Fat and Fierce* (2019), edited by Angie Manfredi, is an intersectional celebration of fatness told in essays, stories, poems, artwork, and fashion tips. The anthology brings together prominent YA and middle-grade authors, social media influencers, and activists. A clear aim of the collection is empowerment, with the narratives acting as a guide for its readers, as Angie Manfredi states, in the introduction, 'I have always believed that when we learn to accept our bodies the way they are – when we learn to love ourselves exactly as we are in the immediate moment – it can shift the world' (p.2). Unlike the books Averill's (2016, p.20) analyses, which centre on books about girls and women who are 'straight and white, and usually either middle class or wealthy', this anthology takes an unequivocal intersectional approach, exploring the experiences of fat-phobia and fat oppression from a variety of perspectives. The anthology thus aligns more closely with Averill's assertation that 'empowerment must be linked to the complex and intersectional nature of true or genuine social justice' (p.15). S. Qiouyi Lu explicitly addressed this, and their experiences about being fat, non-binary, and Asian, in their essay, 'Fat, And.': 'when fat spaces are defined by a standard of experience created by one dominant group – fat and white, for example – other experiences are quick to be pushed aside. I'm not fat for an Asian person; I'm fat and Asian' (p.45). While YA author Isabel Quintero, in her essay, explains how her light-skin privilege, as a light-skinned Mexican American, influences how she is perceived as a fat person: 'this fucked up privilege allows me to let the Mexican jump out, to be more myself, more "weird," more "quirky," more "different" without the same kind of repercussions (being silenced, omitted, rejected) because that light-skinned part of me has already been accepted' (p.112). The anthology also explores how switching between different cultural and ethnic spaces impacts young people's relationships with bodies. In 'Chubby City Indian', Lakota author and comedian Jana Schmieding details her childhood, in a small town in Oregon, which was demarcated by two sides of the river. On the white side of the river, where Schmieding went to school, her experiences were dominated by whiteness and her body was considered through white and male gazes; something that she began to internalise alongside the desire to be accepted. On the Indigenous side of the river, she danced alongside other Indigenous women of all shapes and sizes and felt a sense of affirmation, kinship, and belonging, whilst understanding the sacredness of her own body: 'My bigness and boldness on the dance floor were a celebration of their courage and endurance in the face of so much historic silencing' (p.12). Published two years later, *Every Body Shines: Sixteen Stories about Living Fabulously Fat* (2021), edited by Cassandra Newbould, also focuses on fat protagonists pushing back against tropes and stereotypes, with stories about body diversity and fat acceptance. Compared to *The (Other) F Word* – which has more of an empowering, pedagogical approach – the works of fiction in *Every Body Shines* really focus on how the main characters deal with fatphobia from friends, family, and society in general. There are several stories that include restrictive dieting techniques (e.g. calorie counting) and where the protagonists have internalised fat phobia. Both 'Dupatta Diaries'/Nafiza Azad and 'Food Is Love'/Chris Baron have characters who love and enjoy food but are body-shamed by family members so restrict their diets (or have restricted diets forced upon them). This leads to self-loathing, complicating their love of food, as we can see from Jamilah's experience in 'Dupatta Diaries', 'Butter chicken has too many calories, and I, having the audacity to be fat don't have the right to eat it' (p.72), and Josh's questioning in 'Food is Love', 'How is food love when every bit I take is eye-rolled and examined by my own grandmother?' (p.93). Overall, these two anthologies explore how various fat authors and artists perceive their bodies and navigate the world, and act as a type of 'knowing kinship' with the aim of resisting gendered and racialised fatphobia (Kost & Jamie, 2023). However, *The (Other) F Word* aligns more with Byers' (2018) contemplation, 'Perhaps that is the next step for fat characters in YAL: imagining worlds filled with complex, intersectional characters whose communities exist beyond thin-thinking and fat-hate' (p.168).

Disability and Mental Health

Historically disabled people were not given the opportunity to share their stories (Hall, 2015). Consequently, stories with disabled characters were written by non-disabled people, which, oftentimes, created and/or perpetuated some of the stereotypes about disabled people that still exist today

(Dunn, 2014). Disability was often portrayed in stereotypical and negative ways, reflecting societal misconceptions and fear (Hall, 2015). In the mid-twentieth century, the portrayal of disability began to shift, with some authors starting to explore more complex and nuanced depictions of disabled characters. However, stereotypes and ableism persisted in many narratives. In response to the growing Disability Rights movement in the 1970s, Biklen and Bogdan (1977) undertook an investigation into how disability was portrayed in a corpus of classic literature and other popular media. They identified ten main stereotypes that were used to portray disabled people: pitiable and pathetic; the object of violence; sinister and/or evil; used as 'atmosphere' (i.e. as a prop to the main character or story); 'super crip' (e.g. having superpowers or being an overachiever); laughable; maladjusted-own worst enemy; burden to family/society; asexual; and unable to live a successful life (Biklen & Bogdan, 1977). Despite this problematic positioning of disabled people for decades there has been, more recently, a push for more culturally authentic books by and about disabled people (Brown, 2020).

YA has started to embrace intersectionality, showcasing disabled characters who are also part of other marginalised groups. These stories address not only physical disabilities but also mental health, neurodiversity, and chronic illnesses. *Unbroken: 13 Stories Starring Disabled Teens* (2018), edited by Marieke Nijkamp, is one of these interventions. As the title suggests, this multi-genre anthology of thirteen stories features disabled characters written by disabled authors.[20] The characters in these stories span different disabilities, 'races'/ethnicities, gender identities, and sexualities.

Some of the stories touch upon some of the aforementioned disability stereotypes or the explicit or internalised ableism the disabled characters encounter. For example, in 'Britt and the Bike God'/Kody Keplinger, the main character Britt has retinitis pigmentosa, which results in her going blind. Throughout the story Britt navigates her disability, especially as an

---

[20] Kody Keplinger, Kristine Wyllys, Francisco X. Stork, William Alexander, Corinne Duyvis, Marieke Nijkamp, Dhonielle Clayton, Heidi Heilig, Katherine Locke, Karuna Riazi, Kayla Whaley, Keah Brown, and Fox Benwell.

avid biker, and discusses her concerns about being a burden to her friends and family. All of this takes a mental and physical toll on Britt:

> Being a burden was the last thing I wanted. I felt like one a lot since losing my sight. Like I was inconveniencing the people around me. I felt like I was constantly working my ass off to keep up, to require as little assistance as possible. Not just in cycling, but every day. It was exhausting. (p.47)

'Inspiration porn' – showing disability as an obstacle that can be overcome for the non-disabled gaze – and bravery is also touched upon in the story (Young, 2012). Britt states, 'I hated being called brave. It was almost as bad as inspiring' (p.35). Grue (2016) argues that the inspirational narrative around disabled people is problematic because it (a) objectifies disabled people, whilst assuming that the audience for these images or narratives is non-disabled; (b) devalues disabled people by highlighting simple acts (Grue gives the example of walking on prosthetic legs), which downplays disabled people's scope for achievements; and (c) individualises disabled people. Disability is seen as a personal hurdle, ignoring systemic causes. The story, however, does not centre on Britt's blindness; instead, it has romance at its core. In addition to the aforementioned tropes and stereotypes around disability, the 'magic cure' trope (an extension of the 'super crip' trope) has been prevalent in many fantasy and science fiction narratives. This trope entails a disabled character experiencing a magical or miraculous healing of their disability or gaining a supernatural ability that nullifies their disability, thereby portraying them as 'complete' within the context of the story (Stemp, 2004). Heidi Heilig addresses, and subverts, this trope in 'The Long Road', which follows a disabled protagonist, Lihua, and her family on a lengthy journey towards Persia with the belief that a cure awaits them. During their travels, Lihua wears several magical, protective amulets to ward off evil. However, Heilig diverges from the trope. Instead, she takes a different narrative path, allowing her character to gradually recognise that the concept of 'the cure' is problematic. Through her journey and the discovery of a disabled community, Lihua begins to re-evaluate everything she had long considered as truth, as we see through her encounter with another disabled girl, who does not wear numerous amulets:

> 'do you want to know what helps me most? More than amulets, more than clean living?' I look up at her then, meeting her eyes. 'Yes. Please.' 'Talking. Finding others like me. You'll meet more on the journey.' (p.15)

This encounter compels the protagonist to understand that she saw her body as something to be 'fixed', drawing upon the medical model of disability, and leads her to question the notion of normalcy. Lihua comes to realise that bodies are far more intricate than her family had led her to believe.

Mental health, the focus of 'The Long Road', is an important topic in YA (Richmond, 2018). The number of people – including young people – with mental health conditions is rising, especially with the increased use of social media and because of the global COVID-19 pandemic (Creswell et al., 2021). Stigma around mental health issues persists, and so the growing number of books and anthologies on the theme of mental health provides a welcome antidote to this. *(Don't) Call Me Crazy: 33 Voices Start the Conversation about Mental Health* (2018), edited by Kelly Jensen, comprises thirty-three chapters, with each chapter authored by an individual sharing their personal experience, insights, and the path they have taken to effectively manage their mental illness. The anthology reclaims the term 'crazy' and offers profound insights into the daily struggles that individuals confront, and how they are not defined by their mental health. As noted in the introduction: 'There is power in language, and there's power in what a word or label can mean to each person. "Crazy" is not a singular – or definitive – experience' (p.1).

Heidi Heilig, the aforementioned-author of 'The Long Road', explores the concept of the 'cure' again in her essay 'What we're born with and what we pick up along the way' in *(Don't) Call Me Crazy*. As a bipolar person, Heilig writes about how she feels like 'A Bad Crazy' for opting not to medicate or pursue a 'cure' for her illness at this present time. Another interesting essay is 'What I know and what I don't know' by 'Queer Latina Feminist Mental Health Activist' Dior Vargas (diorvargas.com, 2023). It explores the intersection between ethnicity and mental health – the double stigma of being BIPOC and having a mental illness – and the difficulties that come with occupying those different identities. There are still significant stigmas surrounding mental illness: these can create barriers that prevent individuals from seeking help and support. The impact of this stigma is worse for racial and ethnic minorities compared to their white counterparts, due to additional societal hardships such as poverty and discrimination within various policies and institutions. This can compound the difficulties BIPOC face in accessing services (Eylem et al., 2020). In her essay, Vargas argues that mental health is often thought of as a white issue. White adolescents, for example, were more likely than their BIPOC counterparts to self-identify has having a mental illness; however, the psychology workforce is predominantly white (Moses, 2009; APA, 2022). Consequently, Vargas' advocacy for the increased representation of BIPOC in the mental health field and her sharing of educational resources, personal stories, and information related to mental health in BIPOC communities help to normalise conversations around mental health and provides valuable resources for young people who may be struggling.

It's Not OK to Feel Blue (and other lies): Inspirational People Open Up about Their Mental Health (And Other Lies) (2019), edited by Scarlett Curtis, was published specifically to combat the stigma associated with mental health as Curtis establishes in her introductory chapter:

> The shame is the part that twists and turns inside you until it becomes an aching, rotting mass – too painful for one person to carry and too toxic to be explained. The shame is one of the things that can kill. The shame is one of the things that this book hopes to fix. (p.5)

Part of the normalising process is featuring writing from high-profile authors, actors and actresses, social media personalities, activists, and politicians such as the singer and songwriter Sam Smith, supermodel

Naomi Campbell, television personality Davina McCall, and actress Emilia Clarke.

Gendered and racialised barriers are addressed in more depth in this anthology. In 'Saying my mind', Kelechi Okafor talks about her struggles with mental health, particularly as a Black woman and as someone from Nigerian heritage. She notes,

> When I mentioned to my family that I would be seeking therapy, I was told that it was a futile thing to do because 'Nigerians don't suffer from depression' and if I felt depressed it was because I 'wasn't trusting God enough'. I know that many Black people across cultures hear similar things when they consider seeking support for their mental health. (p.175)

As well as highlighting issues within the Nigerian community, Okafor writes about the link between racism and mental health issues; something that numerous scholars have explored (Paradies et al., 2015; Wallace et al., 2016; Schouler-Ocak et al., 2021). Okafor, and Schouler-Ocak et al. (2021), discuss the importance of mental health care professionals, such as therapists, having cultural competency: Okafor's engagements with Black women therapists were 'life changing' after seeing white therapists who often minimised her experiences of racism such as micro-aggressions.

On the other end of the spectrum, white men can also have a conflicting relationship with their mental health. Singer James Blake highlights in his essay 'How Can I complain?' how toxic masculinity is not only detrimental to boys'/men's mental health, but it can also make them reluctant to speak about it or seek professional help:

> From systemic toxic masculinity ('Boys don't cry', basically) and an ostensibly homophobic fear of sensitivity being beer-bonged into us by our friends, family and the media from as early as we can remember [. . .] to the slow realization as we get older that the world is actually stacked towards our success, we end up thinking that our individual psychological decline is shameful. (p. 325)

Factors such a racial and gendered privilege also contribute to unwillingness to self-label:

> I'm still not sure I fully believe I am entitled to be depressed
> or sad at all, because I'm white and cisgender and male, and
> life for people like me is undoubtedly the easiest of any group
> [. . .] I think it's worth examining why many privileged white
> men can end up feeling they have no legitimate claim to pain,
> and then never deal with what they can't lay claim to. (p.323)

The candid and vulnerable discussions in these two anthologies are helpful in dismantling the stigma associated with mental health and mental illness. The substantial number of contributors in *It's Not OK to Feel Blue (and other lies)*, including celebrities, shows that society is gradually progressing towards more meaningful conversations on these topics.

Genre

As inclusive stories move away from 'issue books'/'problem novels', there has been an influx of books written by and/or featuring socially marginalised people across a variety of genres in the YA market.

Romance is one of the most popular and lucrative genres of fiction in the UK and the US (Mohammed, 2019). The genre has also been embedded in the history of YA since its early days. In the 1940s and 1950s, there were many light romance novels that 'dealt almost exclusively with white, middle-class values and morality' (Nilsen & Donelson, 2009, p.61; Cart, 2016). Early romance novels for adults also centred on white, mainly middle-class, women: a trend that has continued, to some extent, to this day (Beckett, 2019). While these YA romances fell out of fashion in the 1960s and 1970s, there was a revival in the 1980s in the form of mass-market paperback series such as *Sweet Valley High* and *Sweet Dreams* (Pattee, 2010; Cart, 2016). Although these were usually written by multiple authors, under one name in the case of the *Sweet Valley High* series, they, again, centred on white, middle-class, cisgendered, heterosexual, non-disabled characters. Anything that fell outside of this was considered niche, as we can see from the history of Black romance books:

> For decades, publishers had confined many black romance authors to all-black lines, marketed only to black readers. Some booksellers continued to shelve black romances separately from white romances, on special African American shelves. Accepted industry wisdom told black authors that putting black couples on their covers could hurt sales, and that they should replace them with images of jewellery, or lawn chairs, or flowers. Other authors of colour had struggled to get representation within the genre at all. (Beckett, 2019)

The spate of dystopian novels featuring romantic storylines that followed in the 2000s – including Stephenie Meyer's *Twilight* series (2005–2008) and Suzanne Collins' *The Hunger Games* trilogy (2008–2010) – purported to represent a more empowered girl protagonist. However, feminist scholars have disagreed as to whether both Bella (*Twilight*) and Katniss (*The Hunger Games*) still embody problematic and stereotypical portrayals of gender (Mann, 2009; DeaVault, 2012; Lem & Hassel, 2012; Montz, 2012; Green-Barteet & Montz, 2014). For example, *Twilight*, which falls under the paranormal romance genre, has a strong rhetoric of abstinence throughout it guided by 'the author's strong religious views about sexual abstinence' (Kaveney, 2012, p.220). More recent YA romance moves away from this white heteronormative model, and YA Romance anthologies play an important role in showcasing a range of different type of romantic protagonists and romances. For example, *Meet Cute: Some People Are Destined to Meet* (2018) brings together some very popular YA authors[21] to write short stories about how two people, who will go on to form a romantic coupling, meet for the first time (a key trope in many romance films and novels). The stories in this anthology are wide-ranging and showcase gender identity, racial, body, and

---

[21] These include: Jennifer L. Armentrout, Katie Cotugno, Jocelyn Davies, Huntley Fitzpatrick, Nina LaCour, Emery Lord, Katharine McGee, Kass Morgan, Julie Murphy, Meredith Russo, Sara Shepard, Nicola Yoon, and Ibi Zoboi.

sexuality diversity. *Hungry Hearts: 13 Tales of Food & Love* (2019) is a multicultural collection, edited by Elsie Chapman and Caroline Tung Richmond, which explores the relationship between family, food, and culture. It features YA authors with diverse heritages: Sandhya Menon, S K Ali, Rin Chupeco, Anna-Marie McLemore, Rebecca Roanhorse, Sara Farizan, Jay Coles, Adi Alsaid, Sangu Mandanna, Phoebe North, Karuna Riazi.

Three Sides of a Heart: Stories about Love Triangles 2017, edited by US Fantasy YA author Natalie C. Parker, uses the love triangle trope as springboard for more inclusive stories. The love triangle trope is ubiquitous in romance stories and has been prevalent in YA in the last couple of decades (Lyttle, 2022). The *Twilight* series and the *Hunger Games* trilogy both include love-triangles: Bella choosing between vampire Edward and werewolf Jacob (*Twilight*) and Katniss torn between her childhood best friend Gale and fellow Hunger Games participant Peeta (*Hunger Games*). However, Lyttle (2022) argues that standard love-triangle narratives are when 'a heterosexual, cisgender girl must choose between two heterosexual, cisgender boys', which does not leave much room for different and/or alternative types of relationships. Written, again, by a collection of prominent USYA authors,[22] *Three Sides of a Heart* does attempt to introduce more relationship diversity, in terms of sexuality, race/ethnicity, social structures, and so on. For example, some of the stories – for example 'Omega Ship'/ Rae Carson, 'The Historian, The Garrison, and the Cantakerous Catwoman'/ Lamar Giles, 'Before She Was Bloody'/Tessa Gratton – centre on, or allude to, polyamorous relationships, a type of relationship structure that is not commonly represented in YA (Lyttle, 2022). Lyttle argues that

> polyamory's emphasis on loving relationships, elevating of friendship, and porous boundaries between platonic and romantic connections could crack the oppressive restrictions on love and friendship for the classic love triangle protagonist, ultimately offering her – and all of her readers – an alternative, unfamiliar, but perhaps freer fate.

[22] Renee Ahdieh, Rae Carson, Brandy Colbert, Katie Cotugno, Lamar Giles, Tessa Gratton, Bethany Hagan, Justina Ireland, Alaya Dawn Johnson, EK Johnston, Julie Murphy, Garth Nix, Natalie C. Parker, Veronica Roth, Sabaa Tahir.

Finally, more recent YA romance anthologies, such as *Fools in Love: Fresh Twists on Romantic Tales* (2021) and *Serendipity: Ten Romantic Tropes Transformed* (2022), offer fresher interpretations of romance tropes. Edited by USYA authors Ashley Herring Blake and Rebecca Podos, *Fools in Love* was originally conceived as an idea on Twitter (now X) when Podos tweeted, 'Is there a YA romcom anthology where each author tackles a different popular trope? I want one' (Podos, 2019). This led to the editors crowdsourcing a list of popular tropes (enemies to lovers, fake-dating, love-triangles, etc.). The anthology authors[23] then chose one of the tropes to centre their short-stories on. This multi-genre, multi-cultural anthology – with stories ranging from fantasy to sci-fi to contemporary – centres LGBTQIA+ characters and relationships. Additionally, one of the stories, Hannah Moskowitz's 'Love Triangle', inadvertently takes Lyttle's (2022) advice and turns the love triangle into a polyamorous relationship. Following a similar concept to *Fools in Love*, *Serendipity: Ten Romantic Tropes Transformed*, as the name suggests, takes ten romantic tropes and transforms them, with a particular focus on more diverse representation. Edited by USYA author Marissa Meyer, whose previous works mainly include retellings of fairy tales, the anthology uses common romantic tropes such as the makeover ('Liberty'/Anna-Marie McLemore), the fake relationship ('Bye Bye, Piper Berry'/Julie Murphy), and forced proximity ('In the Blink of an Eye'/Elizabeth Eulberg).

Some of the aforementioned anthologies feature, or centre on, science-fiction or fantasy stories: genres that have traditionally been dominated by white men (in terms of the authors, characters, and fans). Several scholars of YA have analysed how and why this domination has shaped YA literature. Ebony Elizabeth Thomas (2019) explores how Blackness is reduced to a ghostly background presence in fantasy literature and links the existence of racist tropes, and conventional racism in science fiction and fantasy, to Black readers and their omission from fandoms. Studies by scholars such as Truman (2019), Toliver (2020), and Doyle (2020)

---

[23] Rebecca Barrow, Gloria Chao, Mason Deaver, Sara Farizan, Claire Kann, Malinda Lo, Hannah Moskowitz, Natasha Ngan, Lilliam Rivera, Laura Silverman, Amy Spalding, Rebecca Kim Wells, and Julian Winters.

highlight the importance of speculative fiction on young people in their development of creative and critical thinking and their engagement in difficult topics. These studies also show how speculative fiction can be an effective tool in engaging students in various, often difficult topics such as police violence, white supremacy, climate crisis, gender binary, and other topics related to identity and oppression. This can be seen in *A Phoenix First Must Burn: Sixteen Stories of Black Girl Magic, Resistance, and Hope* (2020) edited by Patrice Caldwell and featuring Black women and gender-non-conforming authors. *A Phoenix First Must Burn* looks at different Black experiences through fantasy, science fiction, and magical narratives; many of the stories address systemic challenges. In 'Kiss the Sun'/Ibi Zoboi draws upon Caribbean mythology, focusing on the soucouyant,[24] and unpacks colourism in Black communities. The story also grapples with the history of colonisation by exploring the impact of whiteness on Black self-image and identity, and the continued oppression of marginalised people and culture through tourism (and the land-grab that comes with it). Colonialism served as a conduit for middle- and upper-class men from Europe and North America to manifest their sexual desires rooted in the racialisation and exoticisation of indivi-duals in the 'Global South' (Rodriguez Garcia et al., 2017). Sex tourism – a booming industry today – has many ethical issues such as the potential for exploitation and trafficking of vulnerable groups including children, the economic gap between tourists and residents, and the reinforcement of racial and gendered stereotypes (Brooks & Heaslip, 2019). Zoboi touches upon this in the story, with the sou-couyants observing, 'They rub their Black bodies with coconut oil for the white tourists at the resort to gawk at and pay good money for [...] That's why the developers want that piece of our island: so they can have their fantasies' (p.222) and focusing on the unequal dynamic between old white men and young Black girls,

---

[24] A soucouyant is a woman during the day but at night can shed her skin and transform into a fireball witch.

> Ha! Old rich white men and the world innocent don't belong
> in the same sentence, Solange. Especially if they're here in
> Kiskeya. We all know they come for holiday to titillate their
> shriveled-up, incompetent loins with the likes of us – Black
> island girls, tender and sweet. (p.229)

Instead of putting Black girls in a position of inferiority; the stories in this anthology, as the subtitle of the anthology establishes, are about Black Girl Magic, centring Black girls in narratives of resistance and hope. For example, 'Gilded'/Elizabeth Acevedo follows an enslaved girl and metalmancer, who struggles between the possibility of buying her freedom from her enslaver or helping her friends with their revolution and fight for freedom. Set in the 1500s, and inspired by the '1521 Santo Domingo Slave Revolt' on the island of Hispaniola (what is now known as the Dominican Republic), the story reflects on the definition of freedom, as well as who interprets its significance and its situational relevance, asking the question: 'Could you live knowing you had a chance to free many more than yourself, but you refused?' (p.42).

Another example of an anthology that reclaims the speculative fiction genre is *A Thousand Beginnings and Endings*, edited by Ellen Oh and Elise Chapman (2018). This collection of fifteen short stories draws inspiration from Asian mythology and folklore, reinterpreted and creatively reimagined by diasporic Asian writers. The strength of this anthology is the diversity of cultures and mythologies explored. For example, 'Nothing into All'/Renée Ahdieh is a retelling of the Korean folktale *Dokkaebi bangmangi (The Goblins' Club)*, 'Daughter of the Sun'/Shveta Thakrar is a feminist tale inspired by stories from the Sanskrit epic *The Mahābhārata*, 'The Counting of Vermillion Beads'/Aliette de Bodard is based on the Vietnamese fairytale *The Story of Tấm and Cám*, and 'Bullet, Butterfly'/Elsie Chapman retells the tragic Chinese legend *The Butterfly Lovers*. Sohn (2019) argues that

> many young adult fictions that are speculative in modality
> and are penned by Asian American writers often involve
> fantastical worlds that seem detached from the racial politics
> and the social contexts that have dominated critical and
> scholarly conversations.

While this is the case for the stories in this anthology – the narratives do not centre on racial oppression and injustice – they are unapologetically Asian, exploring folklore, traditions, and worldviews from non-Western cultures, which is a subversive practice in itself. For example, Canadian novelist Larissa Lai outlines that the reason she writes speculative fiction is to 'distinguish the racist figurations of Asians in speculative fiction from the work of re-subjectivation in which racialized people reclaim or remake racist stereotypes for the purposes of self-empowerment' (Lai, 2020, p.3). This allows socially marginalised authors to build 'new, freer worlds from the mainstream strain of science fiction, which most often reinforces dominant narratives of power' (Imarisha et al., 2015, p.4). While the positioning of socially marginalised authors in speculative fiction has seen some improvements in recent years, white men still have the upper hand as the racial pay disparities between white and Black science fiction authors suggest (see, for example, #Publishingpaidme) (Flood, 2020). As such, anthologies such as *A Phoenix First Must Burn* and *A Thousand Beginnings and Endings* help challenge the historical hegemony of whiteness in speculative fiction and bridge the 'imagination gap' for young readers (Thomas, 2019).

Activism and Resistance

This chapter has highlighted the vibrancy in YA anthologies and has demonstrated that, especially in recent years, their willingness to challenge white, cisgendered, non-disabled, heterosexual, thin-thinking normativity. As noted earlier, the publishing industry – and its cultural output – has, historically, promoted and supported this type of normativity, so writing and publishing against the grain can be seen as a type of activism. Activism is important for young people, who are now more socially conscious than ever before (Carnegie, 2022). In addition to the growing demand for inclusive and diverse literature – that reflects the changing nature of young people's identities – there have also been anthologies that explicitly call for action or highlight stories of resistance and activism. This chapter will end by highlighting some of the Activism-focused anthologies, centring on issues pertinent to young people today.

Since the #MeToo movement several Feminism-themed anthologies aimed at young people have been published. A core component of contemporary feminism revolves around the necessity of introducing young women to feminist concepts and knowledge. Fernandez and Wilding (2003) assert that equipping young women with exposure to feminist discourse provides them with essential resources to combat the discrimination they encounter in their personal experiences. *Here We Are: Feminism for the Real World* (2017), edited by Kelly Jensen, brings together forty-four people – including writers, actors, and artists of different races/ethnicities, gender identities, sizes, backgrounds and so on – to create essays, poems, illustrations, comics, and other creative outputs. Krestyna Lypen, editor at Algonquin Young Readers (the anthology's publisher), described it as 'a book that's in many ways an introduction to feminism to offer to curious readers' (Patrick & Reid, 2021). Importantly, the anthology takes a fluid approach to feminism, as Malinda Lo outlines in her opening essay: 'Feminism is about recognizing power and fighting to distribute it equally, regardless of race or class or ability or gender. Feminism is not static, and it never has been. In fact, feminism demands change' (p.6). This intersectionality is also the core ethos of *Our Stories, Our Voices: 21 YA Authors Get Real about Injustice, Empowerment, and Growing Up Female in America* (2018), edited by Amy Reed. This is a non-fiction anthology, whose essays explore how gender identity intersects with race, religion, and ethnicity, and it was written with the intention of being a mirror for the readers:

> I hope you read these pages and see yourself in our stories, see that there is a place for you, with us [. . .] I hope you see in the diversity of our stories a common light, a shared humanity and dignity, a community that includes you and the people you care about. (p.x)

The essays have an empowering, and political, undertone with the overarching message, as written in 'Unexpected Pursuits: Embracing My Indigeneity and Creativity'/Christine Day, 'Never dismiss your own perspectives. Never question the validity of life in the margins' (p.50).

The last anthology in this chapter – *Take the Mic: Fictional Stories of Everyday Resistance* (2019) – focuses on everyday acts of resistance and activism; the small, often subtle actions that individuals take in their daily lives to challenge or address societal injustices and promote positive change. As Bethany Morrow outlines in the introduction,

> I thought of the many ways teenage years involve feeling out of control, especially before you even have the option of voting. But I thought too of all the times I'd felt offended, confused, and silent, in the company of so-called friends. I thought about the death by a million cuts young marginalized people often suffer that marching in an organized protest doesn't really alleviate or address [. . .] I won't try to dissuade a young activist from taking to the street in an organized resistance, but I also won't ever tell a marginalized kid that they aren't resisting, that they aren't struggling, that their continuing on isn't enough. (p.x)

These anthologies are responding to a growing trend of civil and political activism among individuals who believe their voices have been disregarded by those in positions of power (Young Women's Trust, 2019). Stories about activism serve as a powerful tool for educating, inspiring, and empowering young people who feel marginalised or unheard. Anthologies do not need to be explicitly about activism/activist movements to do this. The anthologies detailed in this chapter, and the *A Change Is Gonna Come* anthology explored in Chapter 3, have the potential to equip young people with knowledge, empathy, and the motivation to engage in meaningful social and political change. The following chapter builds upon the ideological-representational work YA anthologies do to address intersectional ideas about identity and the representation of socially marginalised, particularly BIPOC, authors in publishing. However, it also illustrates that such anthologies go beyond representation and inclusion: they facilitate community building and solidarity among authors and readers from socially marginalised groups. In this way, anthologies contribute to the formation of resilient, interconnected communities that resist marginalisation and advocate for systemic change.

3 Be the *Change* [book]

This chapter contextualises the previous discussions within British YA (UKYA) focusing on the *A Change Is Gonna Come* anthology; the first UKYA anthology to explicitly bring together BPOC authors. The anthology was commissioned in response to the lack of 'BAME'[25] authors in British publishing, as the commissioning editor, Ruth Bennett, who was interviewed for this Element, outlines:

> There are many great writers of colour who have overcome obstacles to become published and they don't always get the attention and recognition they deserve. However, we knew that there are many more talented writers out there, struggling to get that vital first break in their writing career. We wanted to provide an opportunity for these writers to have their work read and their talents recognised.

While practices surrounding issues of inclusion and exclusion in British publishing have progressed, slightly, since the publication of *A Change Is Gonna Come*, this case study of the anthology provides a useful insight into some of the interventions and advocacy that happened during a critical point in the movement. Through ten semi-structured interviews, the case study uncovers the intricate relationships, contextual factors, and unique patterns shaping the creation of the anthology. This sheds light on how *A Change Is Gonna Come* transcends mere text, fostering a collaborative community that empowered anthology authors and the independent publisher to challenge cultural hegemony in the UKYA market. There were twelve authors/poets included in the anthology: eight established and four new. Seven authors/poets were interviewed for this research, including four established (Catherine Johnson, Nikesh Shukla, Irfan Masters, and

---

[25] BAME is a catch-all acronym for Black, Asian, and minority ethnic people. It is an outdated term that does not consider the different outcomes and discriminations faced by different groups within the term. It was a commonly used term in the UK when the anthology was published but is not used widely nowadays.

Patrice Lawrence) and three new (Mary Bello, Aisha Bushby, and Yasmin Rahman). Interviews were also conducted with Ruth Bennett (Commissioning Editor), Aa'Ishah Hawton (Shadow Commissioning Editor), and Paul Coomey (Art Director) to understand the publishing process. These interviews took place in 2019, so updated information about how 'diversity' is considered in British publishing has been included.

Book Overview

A Change Is Gonna Come (commonly referred to as *Change* book) is a multi-genre YA anthology interpreting the theme of change; it includes short stories and poems. The anthology was published in 2017, during a turbulent cultural moment in the UK, just over a year after the 2016 United Kingdom European Union membership referendum. Brexit exposed rifts between different cultural and ethnic groups in the UK: studies have since linked the vote to leave with xenophobia and prejudice, whilst other studies have noted the rise in racism post-Brexit (de Zavala et al., 2017; Booth, 2019). Whilst the purpose of the anthology is to represent and celebrate 'diverse' ('BAME') voices and cultural identities, authors were given the freedom to interpret the theme however they were inspired to do so. There was a sociopolitical agenda behind the project, but the book itself is intended to have wide appeal for a YA readership, with pieces varying in style and genre. As Ruth Bennett, the Commissioning Editor, expressed:

> Publishing relies on the writing talent and the diversity of voices and stories we publish are what keep the industry alive and thriving. It's important that all readers have access to stories that resonate with them and in order for us to successfully achieve that as publishers, we must constantly be seeking out new voices – especially those that are currently underrepresented by the industry [. . .] Publishing is hugely competitive – so many new books are published every year, and it can be hard for new and unpublished authors to get attention. We wanted to play an active role in helping to give new talent a voice, presenting them in an

anthology alongside established writers and presenting their stories to readers side-by-side with writing from authors they might know already.

Change solicited content from the public in the form of a competition, which is reminiscent of anthology practices of the past. In the Restoration period, readers offered poems for booksellers/editors to include in anthologies while periodicals in the early eighteenth century solicited content from the public (Benedict, 2003). This open and collaborative process is more egalitarian than traditional submissions practices, which increasingly favours agented authors. Since BIPOC authors are less likely to be represented by a literary agent than their white counterparts, competition-driven anthologies such as *Change* offer new and emerging authors opportunities for discovery (Ramdarshan Bold, 2019b). Eight established authors – Tanya Byrne, Inua Ellams, Catherine Johnson, Patrice Lawrence, Ayisha Malik, Irfan Master, Musa Okwonga, and Nikesh Shukla – were invited to contribute and an open competition was held for previously unpublished authors. Four new authors – Mary Bello, Aisha Bushby, Yasmin Rahman, and Phoebe Roy – were selected from over 100 submissions. Ruth Bennett said of the process:

> For the established authors, we created a list of UK writers with a level of profile in the YA market and presented the project to them to gauge interest and availability. We wanted to represent a range of experiences and writing styles. For the emerging writers, we did an open call for submissions, which were then discussed and narrowed down by the Stripes editorial team alongside an industry panel to choose the final four writers whose stories were included [. . .] The open submissions reconfirmed our belief that there is a wealth of undiscovered voices just waiting to be found [. . .] We are delighted to be able to use *A Change is Gonna Come* as a platform for introducing these talented new writers to YA fans.

It is useful, in the context of *Change* book, to think of anthologies as a genre in themselves, even if the authors, genres, and content across different anthologies diverge widely. As Benedict asserts,

> Even while anthologies advertise difference, they paradoxi-
> cally assert similarity. Because of their corporative means of
> production and multiple authorship, anthologies are mate-
> rial expressions of a kind of community, and their format
> also directs readers to understand them as vessels of
> a common enterprise, even while registering the indepen-
> dence of each other. (2003, p.242)

While the shared identity (of being 'BAME') is what tied the authors together, the anthology is not an identity-based narrative, and does not construct one singular identity based on these demographic parameters. Covering genres from contemporary to historical fiction to magical realism to dystopia, the stories span themes/topics such as: hopeful first-love ('Hackney Moon'/Tanya Byrne), living with OCD ('Marionette Girl'/ Aisha Bushby), grief and heritage ('Dear Asha'/Mary Bello), coming-of-age ('Iridescent Adolescent'/Phoebe Roy), far-right extremism post-Brexit ('We Who?'/Nikesh Shukla), the life of a (real-life) Black circus perfor-mer/owner in the early Victorian era ('Astounding Talent! Unequalled Performances!'/Catherine Johnson), the impact of Anti-Muslim sentiment post-Terrorist attacks on Hijab-wearers ('Fortune Favours the Bold'/ Yasmin Rahman), time-traveling ('The Unwritten Future of Moses Mohammad Shabazz Banneker King'/Irfan Master), an unexpected friend-ship in a refugee camp ('A Refuge'/Ayisha Malik), and a Dystopian look at prison/justice systems and reality TV ('The Clean Sweep'/ Patrice Lawrence). The anthology is also bookended with two poems. It begins with Muka Okwonga's 'The Elders on the Wall', which challenges young readers to shape their own destinies and champion change, irrespective of the opinions held by older generations. The poem encourages the idea of independent decision-making while also stressing the importance of joining forces with like-minded individuals on a shared journey towards transfor-mation. The closing poem 'Of Lizard Skin and Dust Storms' by Inua Ellams takes a more reflective tone, conjuring images, and transitions from the past. It considers the conflicting (lived and imagined) lives with which many diasporic communities grapple.

Publishing on the Fringes

The Editorial Process

The role of the editor in the anthology cannot be overstated. Editors shaped how anthologies grew and were seen in the nineteenth century; they were regarded as important cultural tastemakers, selecting contents from the public sphere into a curated collection (Price, 2000). This canonisation process, as outlined in Chapter 1, has been exclusionary in the past. While some editors have attempted to make anthologies – including prominent ones such as Norton's – more representative, they often select canonical authors (e.g. canonical BIPOC authors, of world literature, etc.) rather than less established, contemporary, or new authors (Damrosch, 2006; Prescott, 2016). Independent publishers, such as Stripes in collections such as *Change*, play an important role in circulating such less-established authors.

Editors in contemporary collections of new writing might not have the same type of canonising role; however, their choices still validate the work. They, for example, suggest compiling the anthology in the first place, as Ruth Bennett details the motivation behind the project, 'In my role as a commissioning editor, I was very aware that our publishing was lacking in diversity, and this was something I actively wanted to change'. Editors also participate in the selection process as we saw earlier, and are also involved in bringing a type of paratextual self-awareness to the collection. For example, choosing writer, researcher, and trusted cultural authority, Darren Chetty, to write the foreword brings a certain gravitas to the collection, according to Ruth Bennett, 'Darren is a well-respected figure within publishing and teaching, providing the perfect link between our writers and readers'. This is especially important because, apart from the Shadow Commissioning Editor (which will be explored shortly in this chapter), the Editorial team at Stripes is predominantly white; something that is reflective of the publishing workforce in the UK (Publishers Association, 2023). Consequently, with such gatekeepers, publishing has not been the most welcoming industry for BPOC authors, especially since research outlines the affinity bias editors have with authors who share their cultural background (Childress & Nault, 2018). This led Patrice Lawrence, and a couple of the other authors, to be initially cynical about the *Change* book project:

> I was a little cynical because predominantly white organisa-
> tions 'doing diversity' seems to be trend-led and temporary.
> My agent initially was reluctant for me to agree [to write for
> *Change* book] as I was working full time and juggling
> writing deadlines. However, Ruth seemed really passionate
> about the project, and I like writing short stories. Also – it
> was a short story competition for BAME writers that
> enabled me to find my agent many years ago.

For Ruth Bennett, and the Stripes team, it was not a decision they took lightly, or one to capitalise on a trend, but the opportunity to rethink what their lists looked like and how best to support BPOC authors:

> The hurdles to bringing more diverse voices to the list are
> the traditional routes to publication (editors responding to
> submissions from agents) and the constraints of the identity
> of a list – what is a Stripes book? What is a book we can
> publish and launch successfully? For a relatively small list,
> the progress towards shifting the make-up of the list is
> therefore typically slow and the likelihood is that only one
> or two authors would benefit. The previous year we had
> published *I'll Be Home for Christmas*, a UKYA anthology
> bringing together varied voices. In conversation with the
> Little Tiger Brand Director, we discussed the anthology
> model as an opportunity to champion and showcase the
> range of talented writers of colour in the UK and bring

them to industry and public attention through
a collaborative piece of publishing.

An important aspect of the editorial process for *Change* was the recruitment
of an editorial mentee, Aa'Ishah Hawton, who was the first person to read
through the competition submissions: 'I took the lead on the open submissions process; I had first read of everything that came in.[. . .] It made for
a lot of reading, but I'm so pleased we got as many submissions as we did'
(Aa'Ishah Hawton). Ruth Bennett, and Stripes, made an active decision to
counter the lack of BPOC publishing professionals through this mentorship
activity:

> The lack of diversity in publishing is a staffing issue as well.
> Opportunities to gain experience on meaningful editorial
> projects, and to show your skills, are hard to come by and
> I wanted to use the project as a chance to share my editorial
> experience with an aspiring editor. We received several
> applications and created a shortlist, from which I chose
> Aa'Ishah because of the way she showed her interest in
> and understanding of what is required for an editorial career
> and her aptitude for the role as shown in her application and
> during a telephone interview.

This intervention is important because many BPOC people have, historically, not seen publishing – or the cultural industries in general – as a viable
career path for them, as we can see from Aa'Ishah's experience:

> Growing up I hadn't realised publishing was an area I could
> get into. It was something I gradually became aware of –
> through reviewing and blogging, following authors and
> publishers on social media – but as soon as I knew about
> it, I knew I wanted to be part of it. And for me, editorial felt
> like an instant fit. I knew I'd try and get as much experience
> as possible to help get my foot in the door – and working in
> different departments is always great because it's an insight

Publishing and Book Culture

into the bigger process – but editorial was always my ultimate goal.

Since working on *Change*, Aa'Ishah has an Editorial role at independent publisher, Canongate. Reflecting on her time as a mentee on the project, Aa'Ishah surmised:

> The role of editorial mentee in this particular context [. . .] is (to my knowledge) an unusual one, or at least it was back then. Aside from the book itself, the draw factor of that role was definitely being granted access to, and participation in, the more exciting parts of working in editorial. But I think whatever shape the role takes, it's important both for personal and professional development. They allow more people to see more of the process and can open doors, especially if that person is from a marginalised background. Editorial is known for being the most competitive area in publishing, so anything that can help make it more accessible is useful.

The inclusion of a shadow editor, as we can see from this quote from Ruth Bennett, showed that Stripes were committed to inclusion beyond the product:

> Improving diversity in the publishing industry isn't just about the books we produce; it's about the workforce, too. We wanted to offer a flexible and in-depth placement, allowing a talented future editor to get real experience of the book-publishing process, working in a way that would suit their circumstances. Aa'Ishah's perspective on, and her input into, the development of the project has been invaluable.

Nikesh Shukla described this as 'a brilliant move'; however, he added that 'change won't come until you change the senior management'. Developing Aa'Ishah's skillset with the aim of building her up to be a future editorial leader was a key part of this for Ruth: 'By working with Aa'Ishah, I was able to give her an insight into the process of working on a book through the editorial stages and this was a useful stepping-stone as she embarked on her career.' This 'stepping-stone' had a ripple-effect and also enabled Aa'Ishah to help other BPOC people succeed in publishing/authorship:

> Working on a book like *Change* as a publishing professional of colour is so important because you're in a position to make positive change. Of course, the more senior you are the more influence you're able to exert, but at a junior level if you have that kind of opportunity, you have the chance to make an impact. And again, it's also about reaching back a hand. A big part of being a person of colour in publishing – or any marginalised group – with any level of influence is helping others move forward. It's rewarding work in and of itself but is also crucial to making the industry a better place and the range of books more varied, interesting and reflective of wider society. Working on a project like *Change* means championing voices similar to yours (if only similar in the way they have been silenced or ignored), listening to and actively catering for markets being side-lined, and proving that there is a thirst for their stories.

[Indie] Publishers

Although editors have a critical role in the curation of an anthology, as detailed earlier, the role of the publisher, and who that publisher is, cannot be underestimated.[26] As LeFevere (1992) asserts,

> publishers invest in anthologies, and publishers decide the number of pages they want to invest in. The 'limitations of

---

[26] It is interesting to note that most of the anthologies discussed in Chapter 2 were published by one of the Big Five publishers. Many were published by HarperCollins.

size' or 'space' ritually lamented in almost all introductions
to all anthologies are not a natural given. Rather, they reflect
the anticipated demands of the marketplace. (p.124)

Marketing and sales can determine how much financial backing a book
receives, which can, in turn, impact the content. Design, for example, is
critical for setting a first impression, and conveying the content of a book, to
potential readers. Publishers are responsible for elements such the book
cover and paratexts, paper and print quality, and format. In *Change*, the
foreword and the introduction shape the book, beyond the status of the
authors and poets included, to become cultural advertisements for 'diverse'
and 'inclusive' writing. The 'Note of the Stories' gives a clear insight into
the autonomy the authors had with their writing: 'The purpose of this
anthology is to give creative space to those who have historically had their
thoughts, ideas and experiences oppressed. As such, we have not censored
the topics covered by our writers' (p.4). To counter any sensitivities, trigger
warnings, a glossary of terms, and resources (for people affected or to learn
more) were included. The book cover has a mainstream look that does not
disclose the ethnicities of the authors; it was the Art Director's intention not
to frame the book as a 'diverse' and thus not exoticise the authors or the
writing:

The stories and poems are not about the how the authors or
characters look or where they are from – if they were, then
that would be communicated by the cover [. . .] I questioned
the inclusion of 'Black, Asian and Minority Ethnic' on the
back cover. It's not that I think that where the authors have
come is not important [. . .] it's more that the terminology is
poor descriptor of how diverse the themes inside the book
are. The stories and the poems explore love, sexuality,
identity, reality and so much more – so why not draw
more attention to this to entice readers, rather than to trying
to categorise or define what connects the writers by using
the political construct of 'race'? What has that got to do with
their talent? If anything, it's their cultural upbringing that

shapes them creatively, and that's going to be as different for a Ghanaian writer and a Gujarati writer as it is for an Irish writer and a Italian one. Or two Ghanaian ones [. . .] I don't think that using a term like BAME or communicating how an author or character looks tells readers what a book is about, nor do I think that the colour of an authors' skin or the place of their or their parents' birth puts them in a particular category of writing talent or forms a thematic link worth communicating.

However, Paul Coomey did decide, in the end, to have 'BAME' on this cover for discoverability reasons:

In the world of people and social media and [. . .] reviews, who this group of authors and poets is does matter, because the people who look like they do and come from the places that they come from are under-represented in publishing, and it is important to show this, to make it visible. So that people can find the writing, and also so that people can see that it's possible to tell their stories in print, if that's how they want to tell them – that print publishing does not have to be exclusive.

Change is also noteworthy for its title, as Darren Chetty outlines in the foreword, since it is named after a song, written by Sam Cooke, which became an anthem of the US Civil Rights movement in the 1960s. This positions the book, and its aesthetic and ethos, as bound to a new generation of readers interested in a more inclusive and just world including the books they read.

The type and/or prestige of the publisher cannot be ignored: a conglomerate publisher will, for example, have a much wider readership than a small/independent press, the finances to publish larger print runs, and the sway to be sold in larger bookshops/bookshop chains. As Lacey (2000) argues, 'Having the most potent publishing brand means that those charming and seductive four words, "The Penguin Book Of . . ." are dangerous too. They imply immense authority and status' (p.336). Therefore, as Frank (2001) surmises, the analysis of anthologies

> Should, wherever possible, be supplemented by an enquiry into the circumstances of the making of the anthology, since exclusions, for instance, sometimes testify not so much to the anthologist's values of perceptions [. . .] but to conditions of copyright, available funds, interference from the publisher, or political censorship. (p.14)

Neoliberal publishing has meant that although 'diversity' and 'diverse' books are being published and promoted, it has often been done in a superficial way. Historically, products addressing or reflecting Otherness have been perceived as niche and therefore unprofitable. Consequently, BPOC authors find themselves exploited by the industry to maximise profitability. As publishers increasingly prioritise profits, they are more likely to align with existing and dominant market preferences. While independent publishers are not the only course of support from the publishing industry, they play one of the largest roles in discovering and nurturing emerging voices due to an open submissions policy. As noted earlier, this is not necessarily an option for larger publishers who rely on literary agents. Consequently, independent publishers have displayed a notable history of launching new authors, especially those from socially marginalised groups.

At the time of publishing *Change*, Stripes/Little Tiger was a minority family owned, independent publishing company. Independent publishers, such as Stripes, have less bureaucratic infrastructure than their larger counterparts, and thus have more involvement with their authors and titles. This is important for BPOC authors, who have faced hostilities in British publishing (Ramdarshan Bold, 2019a), especially when, as Patrice Lawrence explains, these motivations extend beyond the superficial: 'Stripes genuinely cared about this project. They went beyond the talk to actually do something that made a difference to the emerging writers and the readers from diverse backgrounds.' While Nikesh Shukla outlined the thought and care given to the authors and the readers, 'Stripes really cared about it [the anthology] coming out in the right way. They gave the book to start conversations in schools, which was really important. They were respectful of the authors'. The [smaller] size of the organisation also meant that the authors gained more of an insight into the publishing process; something that was especially helpful for the emerging authors, as Mary Bello detailed:

> You got to see what the process was like in an energetic, fun, and fostering manner. The team were so focused on walking us through everything, from the offer to edits, PR build up, the launch, press, book tours and beyond. I learnt so much and I'm forever grateful to everyone at Stripes.

This experience also helped the editorial team at Stripes/Little Tiger, notably Ruth Bennett, rethink and revise their/her publishing ethos:

> I learned that it is possible to have an impact on your industry through your approach to publishing, and that there is a value in publishing innovatively and creatively [. . .] I also learned that this action alone is not enough that the process of achieving a more diverse publishing landscape is still far from where it should be. The work needs to be constant and sustained, and it needs to be fully integrated, from the staff within publishing houses to the writers we publish in all kinds of books, not solely in anthologies.

For the established authors, as articulated by Catherine Johnson, 'It felt like an excellent and more importantly, tangible, step forward.' Many of these established authors had been writing and publishing for decades prior to *Change* and grappled with many issues related to being BPOC in publishing/authorship in the UK. Irfan Masters, for example, acknowledged that while there was a little progress, when the anthology was published in 2017, under-representation was still an issue but not bad as in previous years:

> We've started a conversation that when I was published in 2011 was just beginning. I'm so glad about how we're speaking out and being ourselves and actively supporting one another to get out there. That's different to when I started out. I'm still often the only or one of very few brown faces in any book launch, meeting, conference, room. That is still challenging [. . .] I mean, it's bad now, was bad ten years ago, and was atrocious in the 80s and 90s and non-existent in the 70s. We're approaching 50 years of literally no change in publishing trends for more diverse publishing.

Acknowledging the commercial potential of the book, Masters continued, that the book 'presents an opportunity for other publishers to see that such an anthology can be a success, can create a buzz and can be accessible to a wider audience'. And, according to Patrice Lawrence, that is exactly what *Change* did, in part due to the investment of Stripes/Little Tiger:

> It's well-stocked in mainstream bookshops and the launch was a sell-out – so many people of colour! School librarians have welcomed it, and Stripes did a fantastic PR campaign that could put bigger publishers to shame. I think much of this is down to Charlie Morris and Ruth Bennett who genuinely want to change the story and have focussed so much energy and passion in doing so.

Ruth Bennett also underscored the role that *Change* had, at the time of publication, in advancing conversations about 'diversity' in publishing.

> The reaction to the book was wonderfully positive, which I expected because I knew the talent of the writers involved [. . .] The surprising part was the amount of discussion it generated within the industry – I think that it brought the

conversation about ways to address the lack of diversity in publishing for children to the front of people's minds. We presented a book that included work by twelve fantastic writers. When faced with that, it's harder to resort to the argument that the writers aren't coming to you or that the talent isn't there.

While emerging authors are now writing in a different publishing landscape than the established authors, forms such as short stories, as will be discussed shortly in this chapter, and formats such as anthologies allow emerging authors to hone their craft and gain visibility in a crowded market.

Emerging Authors

Benedict (2003) argues that an anthology's success lies with the variety in content rather than the author or the publisher. A key characteristic of the early anthology, in the seventeenth century, was its heteroglossia – the multiplicity of divergent voices and opinions – which was something that appealed to the broad range of readers, and a plural society, at a time of political, social, and religious conflict (Benedict, 2003). This aligns with Price's view that anthologies are 'a challenge to prevailing models of authorship' (2000, p.3). While eighteenth-century anthologies recycled literature – something that caused contention between writers and booksellers at the time – anthologies today support new works by both debut and established authors (Benedict, 2003).

Mary Bello detailed how her experience with *Change* was a 'gentle' introduction to publishing, especially considering the experiences her more established *Change* peers had in the past:

> Anthologies allow emerging authors to gently enter the literary world. It can be scary walking into a field where the establishment can feel a little closed off. If you're not connected you can feel a great deal of trepidation trying to enter it and that feeling is magnified when you are a writer of colour because you are already aware that it's tougher to get a book deal coming from a BAME background. The very existence of anthologies like *Change* mean that a safe space is being created for us specifically

> to share our work. There's an immediacy in the openness and
> friendliness of the publishing sphere and 'the fear' of submission
> dissipates.

While these communities can provide a safe space for individuals to share
their experiences and validate each other's feelings, as will be outlined in
this chapter, not all the new authors found this transparency beneficial. In
fact, it had a negative impact on one of the authors: 'It didn't necessarily feel
like I was being told positive things about the industry and I definitely went
into the industry quite defensively.' However, this same author encountered
tensions that BPOC authors have faced in the past, related to discussing
their ethnic background instead of writing:

> The first panel I ever did was a diversity panel, and the chair
> was asking me about *Change* Book, 'So how did your back-
> ground influence your story in Change Book?' I was like 'it
> didn't' because my character's ethnicity has nothing to do with
> the story whatsoever. It's incidental what the background is.
> I had to say that to the person and correct them. (Anon)

Beyond the success of the anthology itself, it is important to examine what
the impact of the project had on the careers of the authors. For example,
Patrice Lawrence stressed:

> Creating an anthology is one thing, but it's what happens
> next that matters in terms of opportunities for the writers to
> network and create opportunities. Stripes set up events to
> promote the book to other writers of colour as well as in
> festivals, such as Cheltenham and Hay. They worked really
> hard to make sure the new authors had maximum coverage.
> Also – the writers actually got paid! Most anthologies expect
> you to do it for love and exposure.

For the new authors, in particular, this opportunity to build relationships
with agents and other industry professionals, in addition to helping develop

their writing, was invaluable. As Aisha Bushy shared, '*Change* Book did help a lot in that it got me out there, agents were circling from that.' While Mary Bello commended,

> *Change* has been so amazing for my writing career. It gave me the confidence to focus on making a success out of my dreams – agents and publishers reached out to me as soon as the book was out! I think it's also sharpened my tools as a writer. Going through the editing process was a wonderful experience. I'm now more methodical and concise with my writing approach.

However, it is important to point out that all the new authors were involved in the publishing industry or writing to some degree before being published in *Change*: Mary Bello was the editor for *OK! Nigeria*; Aisha Bushby was an assistant at a Literary Agency; Yasmin Rahman was the co-founder of the literary magazine *Scrittura*; and Phoebe Roy won a Sceptre Love short story prize, and worked as an editor, publishing assistant, production editor, ghost writer, and features writer. Patrice Lawrence made an important point that the emerging writers already had ambitions to write and already thought authorship was a legitimate career path for them: 'The new writers already had connections within the industry anyway through work and studying. They were relatively privileged in that respect.' This has not always been the case for BPOC authors in the past (Ramdarshan Bold, 2019a, 2019b). The 'new' authors are still involved in writing and publishing to varying extents: Aisha Bushby and Yasmin Rahman are the most prominent of the four. Both have published numerous novels for young people, although Aisha Bushby now writes for a middle-grade audience rather than a YA audience. Yasmin Rahman has written three YA novels since contributing to *Change* book.

Form and Genre

While the UK short story is probably as healthy as it has been in many years, it is still very much a fringe genre. Economies of scale will always preclude major publishers from investing in short stories beyond a certain point, meaning their home will usually be with indie publishers who are less subject to the market demands of commercial book publishing (Power, 2011). In fact, short story collections are often bestsellers for small and independent publishers (Jenny Brown Associates, 2004). As such the number of collections published by mainstream publishers has fallen significantly, but the number of collections published by the independents (including self-publishing) has increased (Jenny Brown Associates, 2004; Malcolm, 2012; Norrick-Ruehl, 2018)

March-Russell (2009) argues that the short story is 'potentially a more dissident form than the major genres' (p.247). This is because, due to their length, short stories can react and respond quickly to social and cultural changes, issues, and trends more than other genres. Anthologies, such as the *Good Immigrant* and *Change*, for example, have been at the forefront at exploring British racialised identities in a post-Brexit world. Hunter (2007) notes that short stories are 'particularly suited to the representation of liminal or problematised identities' (p.138). While Hanson (1989) argues that this format has traditionally featured previously excluded voices, 'losers, and loners, exiles, women, blacks- writers who for one reason or another have not been part of the ruling "narrative" or epistemological/experiential framework of their society' (p.2).[27] The short story form has also been a significant medium in the development and circulation of postcolonial literature (Orsini, 2004; Hunter, 2007; March-Russell, 2009; March-Russell & Awadalla, 2013), world literature (Hafez, 1992; Cooke, 2004; Pravinchandra, 2014), and regional literature (Pearce et al., 2013). However, as scholars have noted, it is not granted the same cultural prestige as other literary genres (Pratt, 1994; Pravinchandra, 2014). This is because, as Pratt (1994, p.97) observes, the form is often regarded, by both writers and readers, 'as a training or practice genre' to the novel, a longer and, ostensibly, more difficult form. Ruth Bennett also noted the differences between contributing to anthologies and writing full-length novels, 'anthologies are not by any means the only way for emerging authors to gain recognition and opportunities, and their success in the trade is typically below that of

---

[27] Just a note to highlight that Hanson's use of the adjective as a noun – that is 'blacks' instead of Black people – is demeaning (and grammatically incorrect).

a traditional single-authored novel'. However, as Norrick-Ruehl (2018) argues, 'For newcomers, a published story is also a business card and proof of quality and literary standing. And book publication is usually only possible after publication of individual stories' (p.53).

Although this Element does not explore readers' responses to *Change*, it is impossible to disentangle anthologies from their readers. Anthologies are, according to Benedict (2003), a readers' genre, rather than a publisher's genre. She argues that anthologies – since they introduced readers to multiple texts by different authors – induced a more critical and comparative form of reading (2003). Anthologies have always provided opportunities for readers: historically, they repackaged long, epic works into more manageable pieces; today, they give a snapshot of an author's work in a saturated market. This is important for readers, and publishers and agents, to discover new writing/authors, as Irfan Masters suggests:

> Anthologies are an opportunity to have your work discovered by readers who then will go on to read more of your work in future. They're a chance to capture the attention of editors and agents by showcasing your writing skill. They open up conversations and opportunities in a slightly different way to the typical agent submission process, where focus is often on a specific project's commercial viability rather than the potential of the writer.

Ruth Bennett, also noting the discoverability aspect for readers, also explained how anthologies help promote innovation in publishing:

> I think for readers, there's a huge value in anthologies as a chance to discover the unexpected. You don't select what you are going to read in the same way that you do when choosing a novel. For publishers, I think it's a valuable way of showing that experimentation and risk taking in publishing is important and can be successful.

The brevity of short stories makes them easily accessible to a wide range of readers, including those with limited time or attention. They can be consumed in one sitting, making them suitable for people with busy schedules or those seeking a quick literary experience. Considering the emergence of the novel in the eighteenth century, Premchand (quoted in Pravinchandra, 2018) argues that 'Novels are read by people who have money, and those who have money also have time. Short stories are written for ordinary people, who have neither money, nor time' (p.198). This argument is, of course, rooted in a specific historical moment and does not consider, for example, serialisation practices in the nineteenth century, cheaply printed materials from around the world, the use of books in schools, and library/borrowing practices. However, it does underscore the accessible nature of the short story. In terms of anthologies, they give readers more control over their reading experience. Readers can choose how they read an anthology: they can decide what order to read the short stories or poems or miss one/some entirely. Consequently, anthologies 'invite readers to participate in the narrative action' (Benedict, 1996, p.212).

Due to their compact nature, short stories provide a platform for authors to experiment with narrative techniques, structure, and style. This experimental approach has led to the development of innovative storytelling methods that can influence broader literary trends. While Benedict (2003) argues that, historically, no genre, or author, is given hierarchy over the others in anthologies, Beevers (2008) found that, 'Of short story collections sold, the majority were by writers best known for genre novels' (p.12). BIPOC authors have had a complicated relationship with genre, as outlined in Chapter 2. At the point that *Change* was published, one of the main arguments used to explain the lack of inclusion in the UK publishing industry was the lack of BPOC authors writing; however, BPOC authors are often restricted to a narrow gap in the market; they are offered the opportunity to write a specific set of racially framed narratives (Saha, 2017; Ramdarshan Bold 2019a). Specifically, many BPOC authors encountered pressure to create works centred on their ethnic or cultural heritage, or to rely on cultural stereotypes, as a prerequisite for getting published or maintaining their publishing careers (Ramdarshan Bold, 2019a). These publications frequently had to address subjects like 'racism, colonialism, or postcolonialism, as if these were the primary concerns of all BAME people' (Akbar, 2017). Whereas white authors are published across genres, BPOC authors have had much less access to a range of genres and less creative freedom. Anthologies, such as *Change*, have, therefore, given BPOC authors the space to experiment en masse. *Change*, and the short story format, according to Irfan Masters, had 'a wide brief, and that suited what I wanted to write [. . .] The editorial process was supportive and allowed me to experiment'. Masters continued,

> I thought being included in the book introduced my writing to new audiences that might read some of the other authors. In terms of personal impact, it allowed me to experiment with form and show readers that I was capable of writing in a different way.

This creative freedom was exciting to many of the interviewees, with emphasis on what authors want to write, rather than what they are expected to write. Patrice Lawrence enthused, 'It shows that talented writers from diverse backgrounds write well and, in every genre, possible', while Nikesh Shukla noted, 'It's given some authors the opportunity to write out of type'. Extending on his previous quote, Irfan Masters surmised, 'you get to see what people want to write about'. Another author summed up the frustration that many of the interviewees (and many BPOC authors have felt in general): 'That is why *Change* book was so great, it wasn't about our oppression, or race-related issues' (anon).

This is important because it normalises everyday experiences of and stories by BPOC people, as Tanya Byrne, one of the *Change* authors, articulates succinctly:

> As a BAME author who writes BAME characters, I'm frequently asked to explain why my books are so unusual. They're not unusual, at least I don't think they are. My books are about teenagers doing what teenagers do, trying to find their place in the world and fucking it up along the way. The fact that some of my characters are Nigerian or

Jamaican or, in the case of my story for the new anthology
A Change is Gonna Come, Guyanese, doesn't make them
unusual. It just means that my books reflect the world in
which we live, as all books should. (Byrne, 2017)

Mirrors and Windows

In the publishing and wider cultural and creative industries, Otherness has
typically been controlled and subjugated through representation. This had
an impact on the authors in *Change*, none of whom really saw themselves in
books as children and young adults. Yasmin Rahman disclosed this was
a motivation for writing:

I write contemporary YA fiction and am determined to
increase the diversity in children's literature. Growing up
as a British Muslim, I could never find any characters that
I felt represented my experiences. Being selected for this
anthology has made me realise that not only is there
a market for stories like mine, there's a need for them.
My mission as a writer is to avoid my nieces and nephews
having the same dilemma.

This mirror, to use Rudine Sims Bishop's (1990) terminology, was clearly
seen throughout the promotional activities for *Change*, as Patrice Lawrence
observed, 'it shows young people from different backgrounds that there
may be a place for them in publishing – this is especially backed up by the
school visits where the Muslim girls' reaction to Yasmin was a joy to see'.
This also showcases the impact of author school visits on marginalised
children, which is an important enabler in making publishing more inclusive
(Ramdarshan Bold, 2019b). The experience was also a very positive one for
Yasmin Rahman, boosting her confidence in a very memorable way:

This is still one of the most amazing parts of my career so
far, this girl came up to me and wanted to speak to me

specifically afterwards. She was a girl in a hijab just like me, and she came up to me and said, 'I just want to say it's really nice to see an author talking about things that you talk about, and writing about things that you write.' I was just like, 'Oh my God!

Such encounters, and representation, is important, especially at such a formative age, as Yasmin describes:

I think at that point every single book was about terrorism, oppression, taking off your hijab, kind of thing, so to have a book where none of that is mentioned and it's a nuanced representation of modern life as a youth in this culture, would have been amazing for sure.

Tanya Byrne is adamant that *Change* was not published, or written, with the archetypal white audience in mind:

A Change is Gonna Come isn't for them, it's for Mary Bello, Aisha Bushby, Yasmin Rahman and Phoebe Roy, the writers who were published in it for the first time. And it's for the Guyanese girl I met at the launch last week who'd never read a book with a Guyanese girl in it and the Muslim guy who'd just come out to his family. It's for the teenagers who want change, who need change, who need to know that, despite the Nazis wielding tiki torches in Charlottesville, they matter. It's for the teenagers who need to know that change – actual, real, demonstrable change – is possible and, despite what we're told, we don't need to wait for it, to be patient and grateful for whatever comes our way. We can be – actually we have to be – disruptive. We have to get in the way, to be heard, be seen. As Chimamanda Ngozi Adichie says, 'You deserve to take up space'. (Bryne, 2017)

While the stories are not told through the white gaze, and are not written for a white audience, the anthology does serve as a window book. Both Sims Bishop's 'Windows' metaphor, and LaCapra's (2001, p.41) model of 'empathic unsettlement' are germane to literature about cultures and experiences outside our frame of knowledge. It represents the middle-ground between narratives that welcome empathy and allow readers to understand different worlds, whilst also demonstrating that there are limitations to our understanding. This model can be applicable to non-BIPOC readers of *Change* book, where some of the stories tackle explicit racism (alongside other forms of discrimination). It can also introduce white readers to stories and poems by BPOC authors that are not centred on ethnicity, or issues of race and racism. This is important because, as Mary Bello, invoking Chimamanda Ngozi Adichie, states, 'Finding voices from all ethnic backgrounds is vital because the world does not revolve around a single story. There are so many rich, wonderful tales that live in the hearts of people from all walks of life. These stories deserve to be heard'.

Consequently, the *Change* authors are creating counternarratives, as Tanya Byrne outlines:

> Real, demonstrable change [...] begins with resistance. Resisting whatever box we're put in, whatever narrative is being written about us. We must tell our own stories and if there is no space for us to do so, then we will make space for ourselves. Like Rupi Kaur did when she self-published *Milk and Honey* and Issa Rae did with her web series, *The Misadventures of Awkward Black Girl*, which now has over 25 million views on YouTube. (Byrne, 2017)

Counternarratives do not replace the prevailing narrative; rather, they provide a platform and an opportunity for marginalised groups to express themselves and gain recognition. Counternarratives prove especially valuable in deconstructing essentialist identities that are constructed by dominant groups. Consequently, these counternarratives challenge dominant viewpoints and stereotypes, ultimately empowering authors and readers from marginalised backgrounds. For the BPOC British authors in *Change* this meant constructing their own notions of Britishness and showcasing BPOC British adolescence. UK publishing has, in the past, depended on imports from the US, particularly books by BIPOC authors. As such, anthologies like *Change*, which look at contemporary British identity, are important. As Tanya Byrne (2017) put it, 'BAME writers must tell their own stories – and we have to be disruptive'. In this sense, anthologies serve as repositories of cultural knowledge and collective memory; through their writing, at this particular moment in British history, the *Change* authors document their communities' traditions, struggles, and triumphs, ensuring that these stories are not forgotten or erased. By valuing and preserving BIPOC (and other socially marginalised) voices, anthologies empower authors to reclaim their narratives and assert their cultural sovereignty in the face of ongoing erasure and cultural appropriation.

Building a Community

A critical part of this research is the relationship between anthologies and community formation amongst BPOC UKYA authors. Community, in this instance, is the network of authors and the institutional frameworks that enable their collaborative work. Factors contained in the anthology eco-system include a culture of support, that is, the means of encouraging, promoting, and supporting authors, particularly those at the start of their careers. Community building has long been an essential activist tool, indeed even in cultural activism, that not only creates opportunities for shared learning and growth but also helps community members leverage their collective resources and visibility to demand change from those in positions of authority (Wakholi, 2017). Community building is particularly important for BIPOC individuals because it provides an empowering space to connect with others who share similar cultural backgrounds, experiences, and struggles (Maton et al., 2011). This sense of solidarity fosters a feeling of belonging and validation, helping to counteract the isolation and marginalisation that BIPOC individuals may face in predominantly white or non-inclusive spaces. All the interviewees emphasised the importance of community and resistance to the elitism and monocultural nature of the publishing industry.

As outlined earlier, being in a community of authors was particularly beneficial to the new authors. The collaborative experience was educational for them, as Yasmin suggests:

> One thing that I can say is that it's prepared me a lot more for publication. Obviously with *Change* Book we had events and tours and things like that, and people coming up to us and signings. It was like a little crash course in being an author, and I think that helped so much when I got to my own publication because I knew what to expect. I knew what to do, I knew what not to do, kind of thing. I knew that it was okay to be terrified.

This training (of sorts) is crucial because authorship can be precarious, and the concentration of the publishing industries has made it difficult for people (particularly BIPOC authors) to join. BPOC authors face common barriers that not only prevent them from pursuing creative careers but can also hinder their careers once they have been published (Ramdarshan Bold, 2019b). Anthologies such as *Change* – and the function of the anthology itself as an important community builder – are important interventions to tackle these systemic problems and inequalities. The underrepresentation of author role models can have a lasting impact on emerging or aspiring BPOC authors: it can indicate that authorship is not a viable career for marginalised groups and that cultural output favours white, middle-class stories, aesthetics, and values. The lack of familiarity with the cultural sector led many of the interviewees to feel uncomfortable and 'out of place' at various publishing events, as we saw earlier when Irfan Masters said, 'I'm still often the only or one of very few brown faces in any book launch, meeting, conference, room'. One of the established authors described the YA community as 'very cliquey' and 'dominated by white women'. They continued:

> YA is very cliquey. It seems like YA is less concerned with teenagers and more concerned with white women writing books that other white women wanted to read in their teens.

> I'm not really interested in being part of a YA clique. I'm
> there to write books for teenagers. (Anon)

Publishing is reliant on networking; however, this can be restrictive for people with no connections in the industry. Therefore, having a ready-made network can help authors, at all stages in their career, combat some of these barriers, including help with negotiating the traditionally white spaces, which BPOC authors often struggle to inhabit. This is something that Stripes/Little Tiger considered when pitching the anthology:

> People often speak about the opacity of the publishing
> industry – lack of understanding is a barrier to entry and
> to successfully navigating the experience of being a new
> author. By creating a support network, it ensures that new
> writers are able to benefit from the knowledge and experi-
> ence of other writers whose advice and insight is likely to be
> far more valuable to them than mine as part of the white
> publishing establishment. (Ruth Bennett)

Irfan Masters acknowledged the role he and the other established authors had, saying, 'I think mentorship, or at least vocal support from established authors of colour is really important in encouraging more writers to get their voices out there. It provides platforms in which to try new things and point to what's already out there and say, I can do this, I can see a way through'. Nikesh Shukla described it as 'a massive comfort. There's that stereotype of "you all know each other" and the hilarity is that it's partly true. It's true because of the impact of being the only people in the room; you do gravitate towards each other'. He continued, 'all the writers of colour know each other. We've brought four more people into the fold'. Two of the new authors, Mary and Yasmin, outline how valuable this can be, and how mentorship was an important part of the *Change* experience:

> *Change* put me in touch with a whole community of writers
> who are incredibly supportive [. . .] entering the literary

world can be a little daunting and knowing that there are people who will genuinely understand you is golden. Also, they give you hope. You know that they made it and maybe you can too. Plus, how phenomenal is it to be able to pose questions to the brilliant, bright, and brave who have walked the path before you? (Mary Bello)

It really helped having the established authors who were doing the events with us. We looked up to them, they were what we wanted to be in a few years' time. They were the font of all knowledge. I think my very first event that I did was with Patrice Lawrence. I was like, oh, she's just won the frigging Waterstones prize [. . .] We did a lot of events with them, and everyone is so nice and willing to answer our questions. We had dinner together and talked to each other, and it was just so nice to see that there could be a place for us [. . .] and that we fit into it without it being weird. They didn't treat us differently because we were new and weren't technically published. (Yasmin Rahman)

One of the new authors, however, was concerned about the ghettoising nature of being in a collection that featured solely BPOC authors:

I think as well that sometimes with *Change* Book, because as much as I'm so grateful having been chosen for that, part of me is like because it was focused on authors of colour, part of me was like am I always going to be 'here is our good authors and here is our good authors of colour.' Am I always going to be compared amongst a smaller pool? I want to be known as an author, not as an author of colour. (anon)

However, Aa'Ishah Hawton countered that anthologies, such as *Change*, were a stepping-stone to a more inclusive publishing landscape:

By doing the work – i.e. by continuing to acquire and publish more diversely and champion diverse authors –

hopefully we can get to a point where we don't need to think
about constructing an anthology solely because the number
of published marginalised authors is so low.

In general, these networks often lead to lasting friendships and
connections, providing ongoing support and camaraderie. For the new
authors, this enabled them to start setting up a peer-support system.
Yasmin outlines:

Funnily enough, Aisha Bushby, who was on *Change*
Book, me and her are best friends now through meeting
through there [...] it's very much like we went on the
absolute same journey, in a way. We got an agent around
the same time [...] we got published in the same year, we
debuted together.

Relationship-building was also important for the more established authors,
as we can see from Patrice Lawrence's experience, 'It did enable me to
deepen friendships with Catherine Johnson and Tanya Byrne'. As we have
seen from the above, both professional and peer-support networks are
crucial for BPOC authors. Anthologies, such as *Change*, can therefore:
provide a safe and understanding environment where individuals facing
similar challenges can share their experiences, feelings, and concerns; boost
self-esteem and confidence; reduce feelings of loneliness and foster a sense
of belonging; and exchange practical information and advice based on their
experiences. This can be particularly helpful when dealing with complex
issues or navigating unfamiliar situations.

Unite and Ignite: The Collective Power of Inclusive YA Anthologies

This Element has outlined the history of anthologies, spotlighting the
politics of YA publishing and the potential of the YA anthology form to
make social change. This historical overview is essential for understanding
contemporary anthologies, especially regarding issues of exclusion, because
it provides context, identifies patterns, traces influences, highlights counternarratives, and informs critical analysis. By contextualising contemporary

anthologies within their historical frameworks, this Element helps scholars and practitioners alike to understand the complexities of exclusionary practices and work towards a more inclusive literary landscape.

Anthologies are instrumental in defining cultural traditions and offer a unique vantage point for engaging questions about multiculturalism and identity politics from different perspectives. Stories in anthologies, such as the ones detailed in this Element, use counterstorytelling as a mode of distancing BIPOC characters, for example, from the dominant ideological constructions of BIPOC. This allows the authors and the anthologies themselves to engage in the process of creating and articulating a new direction for BIPOC characters in young adult fiction. This also works across different socially marginalised identities. For example, intersectionality, the interconnected nature of social identities and systems of oppression, has become a prominent theme in contemporary anthologies. Multi-authored books, such as anthologies, are often better equipped to engage with intersectionality. By bringing together authors from different backgrounds, anthologies such as those outlined in Chapter 2 often explore how factors like race, gender, sexuality, and disability intersect to shape individual experiences. This is important because the 'culture wars' – being fought over LGBTQIA+ rights (especially trans rights), pronouns, racism, abortion rights, free speech etc. – are ultimately contributing to a divided society. Anthologies, therefore, have the potential to have a unifying role, like they did during divided periods in the past (Benedict, 2015). The anthologies in this Element, therefore, cross the boundaries between literature and activism, showing the interconnectedness between narrative, identity, community, and activism.

The focus of this Element's case study – the *Change Is Gonna Come* anthology – and others like it make their agenda explicit, searching for specific viewpoints and contributors. *Change* was conceptualised, commissioned, and published with the clear goal of resisting the cultural hierarchies that have existed in British publishing since its inception. The publisher Stripes are, therefore, doing valuable work by circulating literature that might not have been read widely beyond its context to a YA audience. These shorter narratives are particularly attractive to a younger generation of readers, supportive of marginalised voices, and pivotal in challenging cultural hierarchies in contemporary publishing. In *Change* book, the format gave the authors the possibility of experimenting with genre and not being confined to writing contemporary realism or identity books. Most importantly, it created a wider community of BPOC authors, not only to help each other navigate the often-hostile environment of British publishing, but also to create counternarratives en masse. Community building facilitates collective advocacy and activism efforts aimed at addressing systemic injustices and advocating for social change. By coming together, in *Change*, the authors were able to empower each other, amplify their voices, and leverage collective power to challenge oppressive systems and institutions. The book also had a domino effect for other publishers, as Ruth Bennett surmised, 'After *Change*, I think other publishers may have felt more confident to try anthology publishing, whether it be self-generated or US buy-ins.' *Change* book is therefore at the forefront of influencing British YA publishing practices.

Overall, inclusive YA anthologies, like the ones discussed in this Element, have a unique ability to disrupt traditional publishing norms by amplifying a range of voices, perspectives, and experiences that might not always be represented in mainstream publishing and by building new creative communities. They can introduce new ideas and innovative storytelling techniques into the literary landscape through the cross-pollination of genres, styles, and contributor backgrounds, and provide a space for both established and emerging authors to experiment and take risks. This can make different types of literature more accessible, especially for readers who may not have the time or resources to explore multiple authors or genres individually. Finally, the collaborative aspect of anthologies is a counter to the individualistic nature of traditional publishing, where ideas are often shaped by multiple voices and perspectives but where individual authors, especially bestselling ones, are most valued. Anthology communities are therefore not only sites of resistance but also incubators of cultural and social change. Through collective action, these literary communities can challenge dominant narratives, and oppressive norms and structures, paving the way for more equitable and just publishing industries.

References

Primary texts

Alsaid, A. (ed.) (2021) *Come on In: 15 Stories about Immigration and Finding Home*. New York: HarperCollins.

Blake, A. and Podos, R. (eds.) (2021) *Fools in Love: Fresh Twists on Romantic Tales*. New York: Running Press.

Caldwell, P. (ed.) (2020) *A Phoenix First Must Burn: Stories of Black Girl Magic, Resistance and Hope*. London: Hot Key Books.

Chapman, E. and Tung Richmond, C. (eds.) (2019) *Hungry Hearts: 13 Tales of Food & Love*. New York: Simon & Schuster.

Charaipotra, S. and Ahmed, S. (eds.) (2023) *Magic Has No Borders*. New York: HarperCollins. https://libbyapp.com (downloaded 01 June 2023).

Chase, C. (ed.) (1998) *Queer 13: Lesbian and Gay Writers Recall Seventh Grade*. New York: William Morrow.

Clayton, D. (ed.) (2021) *A Universe of Wishes*. London: Titan Books.

Curtis, S. (2019) *It's Not OK to Feel Blue (and other lies)*. New York: Penguin.

Dane Bauer, M. (1995) *Am I Blue?: Coming Out from the Silence*. New York: HarperCollins.

Dawson, J. (ed.) (2019) *Proud*. London: Little Tiger Press Group.

Fennell, S. (ed.) (2021) *Wild Tongues Can't Be Tamed: 15 Voices from the Latinx Diaspora*. Flatiron Books. Retrieved from Amazon Kindle: www.amazon .co.uk/Wild-Tongues-Cant-Be-Tamed-ebook/dp/B08QGJTH21/ ref=tmm_kin_swatch_0?_encoding=UTF8&qid=1700048504&sr=8-1 (downloaded 15 November 2022).

Giles, L. (ed.) (2018) *Fresh Ink*. New York: Random House USA.

Jensen, K. (ed.) (2017) *Here We Are: Feminism for the Real World*. New York: Hachette.

(2018) *(Don't) Call Me Crazy: 33 Voices Start the Conversation about Mental Health*. New York: Hachette.

Levithan, D. and Merrell, B. (eds.) (2006) *The Full Spectrum: A New Generation of Writing About Gay, Lesbian, Bisexual, Transgender, Questioning, and Other Identities*. New York: Alfred Knopf.

Mandanna, S. (ed.) (2019) *Color Outside the Lines: Stories about Love*. New York: Soho Press.

Manfredi, A. (ed.) (2019) *The (Other) F Word: A Celebration of the Fat & Fierce*. New York: Amulet Books.

Meyer, M. (ed.) (2022) *Serendipity: Ten Romantic Tropes, Transformed*. New York: Macmillan.

Mitchell, S. (ed.) (2018) *All Out: The No-Longer-Secret Stories of Queer Teens throughout the Ages*. New York: HarperCollins.

(2020) Out Now: Queer We Go Again! New York: HarperCollins.

(2022) *Out There: Into the Queer New Yonder*. New York: HarperCollins.

Morrow, B. C. (ed.) (2019) *Take the Mic: Fictional Stories of Everyday Resistance*. New York: Scholastic.

Newbould, C. (ed.) (2021) *Every Body Shines: Sixteen Stories about Living Fabulously Fat*. London: Bloomsbury.

Nijkamp, M. (ed.) (2018) *Unbroken: 13 Stories Starring Disabled Teens*. New York: Farrar, Straus & Giroux.

Oh, E. and Chapman, E. (eds.) (2018) *A Thousand Beginnings and Endings*. New York: HarperCollins.

Parker, N. (ed.) (2017) *Three Sides of a Heart: Stories about Love Triangles*. New York: HarperCollins.

Reed, A. (2018) *Our Stories, Our Voices*. New York: Simon & Schuster.

Various authors (2017) *A Change Is Gonna Come*. London: Little Tiger Press Group.

Various authors (2019) *Meet Cute*. New York: HarperCollins.

Various authors (2021) *Blackout*. New York: HarperCollins.

Various authors (2022) *Whiteout*. New York: HarperCollins.

Zoboi, Ibi (ed.) (2019) *Black Enough: Stories of Being Young & Black in America*. New York: HarperCollins.

Secondary texts

Berland, E. (2017) 'The Drama of Coming Out: Censorship and Drama by Raina Telgemeier'. In Michelle Ann Abate, and Gwen Athene Tarbox (eds.),*Graphic Novels for Children and Young Adults: A Collection of Critical Essays*, University Press of Mississippi, 205–217. https://doi.org/10.14325/mississippi/9781496811677.003.0014.

Akbar, A. (2017) 'Diversity in publishing – still hideously middle-class and white?' *The Guardian* [online], 9 Dec. www.theguardian.com/books/2017/dec/09/diversity-publishing-new-faces. Accessed 15th November 2023.

American Psychological Association (2022) 'Demographics of U.S. Psychology Workforce' [Interactive data tool]. www.apa.org/workforce/data-tools/demographics Accessed 15th November 2023.

Averill, L. (2016) 'Do Fat-Positive Representations Really Exist in YA?' *Fat Studies*, 5(1), 14–31.

Bailey-Morley, A. and Kumar, C. (2022) 'The rise of the far right in Denmark and Sweden – and why it's vital to change the narrative on immigration'. *ODI* [online]. https://odi.org/en/insights/the-rise-of-the-far-right-in-denmark-and-sweden-and-why-its-vital-to-change-the-narrative-on-immigration/. Accessed 15th November 2023.

Banks, W. P. (2009) 'Literacy, Sexuality, and the Value(s) of Queer Young Adult Literatures'. *The English Journal*, 98(4), 33–36.

Banta, M. (1993) 'Why Use Anthologies? Or One Small Candle Alight in a Naughty World'. *American Literature*, 65(2), 330–334.

Barker, M.-J. (2016) *Queer: A Graphic History*. London: Icon.

Baumbach, M., Petrovic, A., and Petrovic, I. (eds.) (2010) *Archaic and Classical Greek Epigram*. Cambridge: Cambridge University Press.

Beckett, L. (2019) 'Fifty shades of white: the long fight against racism in romance novels'. *The Guardian* [online], 4 April. www.theguardian.com/books/2019/apr/04/fifty-shades-of-white-romance-novels-racism-ritas-rwa#:~:text=Some%20booksellers%20continued%20to%20shelve,or%20lawn%20chairs%2C%20or%20flowers. Accessed 15th November 2023.

Beevers, J. (2008) 'What Is the Short Story'. In Ailsa Cox (ed.), *The Short Story*, Newcastle Upon Tyne: Cambridge Scholars, 11–26.

Benedict, B. M. (1996) *Making the Modern Readers: Cultural Mediation in Early Anthologies*. Princeton: Princeton University Press.

(2003) 'The Paradox of the Anthology: Collecting and Différence in Eighteenth-Century Britain'. *New Literary History*, 34(2), 231–256.

(2015) 'Choice Reading: Anthologies, Reading Practices and the Canon, 1680–1800'. *The Yearbook of English Studies*, 45, 35–55.

Bhanot, K. (ed.) (2011a) *Too Asian, Not Asian Enough*. Birmingham: Tindal Street Press.

(2011b) 'Author Interviews: Kavita Bhanot on Too Asian, Not Asian Enough'. *The Asian Writer*. https://theasianwriter.co.uk/2011/10/11/too-asian-not-asian-enough/. Accessed 15th November 2023.

Biklen, D. and Bogdan, R. (1977) 'Media Portrayals of Disabled People: A Study in Stereotypes'. *Interracial Books for Children Bulletin*, 8(6–7), 4–9.

Bishop, R. S. (1990) 'Mirrors, Windows, and Sliding Glass Doors'. *Perspectives: Choosing and Using Books for the Classroom*, 6(3), ix–xi. www.scenicregional.org/wp-content/uploads/2017/08/Mirrors-Windows-and-Sliding-Glass-Doors.pdf. Accessed 15th November 2023.

Blain, V., Clements, P., and Grundy, I. (eds.) (1990) *A Feminist Companion to Literature in English: Women Writers from the Middle Ages to the Present*. London: Batsford.

Bobker, D. (2015) 'Coming Out: Closet Rhetoric and Media Publics'. *History of the Present*, 5(1), 31–64.

Bona, M. (2017) 'The Culture Wars and the Canon Debate'. In D. Miller (ed.), *American Literature in Transition, 1980–1990*, Cambridge: Cambridge University Press, 223–224.

Bond, E. (2019) 'Assembling the Refugee Anthology'. *Journal for Cultural Research*, 23(2), 156–172.

Bonnell, T. F. (2008) *The Most Disreputable Trade: Publishing the Classics of English Poetry, 1765–1810*. Oxford: Oxford University Press.

Booth, R. (2019) 'Racism rising since Brexit vote, nationwide study reveals'. The Guardian, 20 May. www.theguardian.com/world/2019/may/20/racism-on-the-rise-since-brexit-vote-nationwide-study-reveals. Accessed 15th November 2023.

Bravmann, S. (1997) *Queer Fictions of the Past: History, Culture and Difference*. Cambridge: Cambridge University Press.

Brooks, A. and Heaslip, V. (2019) 'Sex Trafficking and Sex Tourism in a Globalised World'. *Tourism Review*, 74(5), 1104–1115.

Brown, G. R. (1988). 'Transsexuals in the Military: Flight into Hypermasculinity'. *Archives of Sexual Behavior*, 17, 527–537.

Brown, M. (2020) '"Tell Me Who I Am": An Investigation of Cultural Authenticity in YA Disability Peritexts'. In Rebekah Fitzsimmons, and Casey Alane Wilson (eds.), *Beyond the Blockbusters: Themes and Trends in Contemporary Young Adult Fiction*, Jackson, Mississippi: University Press, 140–155.

Byers, M. (2018) '"Fats," Futurity, and the Contemporary Young Adult Novel'. *Fat Studies*, 7(2), 159–169.

Byrne, T. (2017) 'BAME writers must tell their own stories – and we have to be disruptive'. *The Guardian* [online], 18 August. www.theguardian.com/books/2017/aug/18/black-and-minority-ethnic-authors-tanya-byrne. Accessed 15th November 2023.

Carnegie, M. (2022) 'Gen Z: How young people are changing activism'. *BBC* [online], 8 August. www.bbc.com/worklife/article/20220803-gen-z-how-young-people-are-changing-activism. Accessed 15th November 2023.

Cart, M. (2016) *Young Adult Literature: From Romance to Realism*. Chicago: ALA.

Cart, M. and Jenkins, C. (2006) *The Heart Has Its Reasons: Young Adult Literature with Gay/Lesbian/Queer Content, 1969-2004. (Studies in Young Adult Literature)*. Lanham, MD: Scarecrow Press.

Cart, M. and Kaywell, J. F. (2018) 'The History of Queer Young Adult Literature'. In Paula Greathouse, Brooke Eisenbach, and Joan F. Kaywell (eds.), *Queer Adolescent Literature as a Complement to the English Language Arts Curriculum*, Lanham, MD: Rowman & Littlefield, 1–8.

Chapman, M. (2017). *Anti-Black Racism in Early Modern English Drama: The Other "other"*. New York: Routledge.

Chester, G. (2022) 'The Anthology as a Medium for Feminist Debate in the UK'. *Women's Studies International Forum*, 25(2), 193–207.

Childress, C. and Nault, J.-F. (2018) 'Encultured Biases: The Role of Products in Pathways to Inequality'. *American Sociological Review*, 84(1), 115–141.

Cohen, R., Newton-John, I., and Slater, A. (2019) '#bodypositivity: A Content Analysis of Body Positive Accounts on Instagram'. *Body Image*, 29, 47–57.

Coleman, R. (2011) 'Roll Up Your Sleeves!'. *Feminist Media Studies*, 11(1), 35–41.

Collins, P. H. (2005) *Black Sexual Politics: African Americans, Gender, and the New Racism*. New York: Routledge.

Cooke, M. (2004) 'Middle Eastern literature'. In Deborah J. Gardner and Jillian Schwedler (eds.), *Understanding the Contemporary Middle East* (2nd ed.), Boulder: Lynne Rienner, 387–423.

Crawford, R. (2023) 'Outbreaks of Poets'. *London Review of Books*, 15 June, Vol. 45, No. 12. www.lrb.co.uk/the-paper/v45/n12/robert-craw ford/outbreaks-of-poets. Accessed 15th November 2023.

Creswell, C., Shum, A., Pearcey, S., et al. (2021) 'Young People's Mental Health during the COVID-19 Pandemic'. *The Lancet*, 5(8), 535–537.

Crisp, T. (2009) 'From Romance to Magical Realism: Limits and Possibilities in Gay Adolescent Fiction'. *Children's Literature in Education*, 40(3), 333–338.

Damrosch, D. (2006) 'World Literature in a Postcanonical, Hypercanonical Age'. In Haun Saussy (ed.), *Comparative Literature in an Age of Globalization*, Baltimore: Hopkins, 43–53.

Damrosch, D. and Spivak, G. C. (2011) 'Comparative Literature/World Literature: A Discussion with Gayatri Chakravorty Spivak and David Damrosch'. *Comparative Literature Studies*, 48(4), 455–485.

de Zavala, G. A., Guerra, R., and Simão, C. (2017) 'The Relationship between the Brexit Vote and Individual Predictors of Prejudice: Collective Narcissism, Right Wing Authoritarianism, Social Dominance Orientation'. *Frontiers in Psychology* 8, 2023.

DeaVault, R. M. (2012) 'The Masks of Femininity: Perceptions of the Feminine in the Hunger Games and Podkayne of Mars''. In Mary F. Pharr and Leisa A. Clark (eds.), *Of Bread, Blood and the Hunger Games: Critical Essays on the Suzanne Collins Trilogy*. Jefferson: McFarland, 190–198.

Di Leo, J. R. (ed.) (2004) *On Anthologies: Politics and Pedagogy*. Lincoln: University of Nebraska Press.

diorvargas.com (2023) 'About'. www.diorvargas.com. Accessed 15th November 2023.

Dolley, C. (ed.) (1967) *The Penguin Book of English Short Stories*. London: Penguin Books.

Dolley, C. (ed.) (1972) *The Second Penguin Book of English Short Stories*. London: Penguin.

Doyle, J. (2020) 'Creative Communication Approaches to Youth Climate Engagement: Using Speculative Fiction and Participatory Play to Facilitate Young People's Multidimensional Engagement with Climate Change'. *International Journal of Communication*, 14, 2749–2772.

Drake, K. (2019) 'When Social Media Goes after Your Book, What's the Right Response?'. *The New York Times* [online], 6th February. www.nytimes.com/2019/02/06/books/amelie-wen-zhao-blood-heir-keira-drake-continent-jonah-winter-secret-project.html. Accessed 15th November 2023.

Duckels, G. (2021) 'Melodrama and the Memory of AIDS in American Queer Young Adult Literature'. *Children's Literature Association Quarterly*, 46(3), 304–324.

Duffy, B., Hewlett, K., Murkin, G., et al. (2021) 'Culture Wars in the UK'. www.kcl.ac.uk/policy-institute/assets/culture-wars-in-the-uk.pdf. Accessed 15th November 2023.

Dunn, D. (2014) *The Social Psychology of Disability*. Oxford: Oxford University Press.

Epstein, J. (2001) *Book Business: Publishing Past, Present, and Future*. New York: WW Norton.

Eylem, O., de Wit, L., and van Straten, A. (2020) 'Stigma for Common Mental Disorders in Racial Minorities and Majorities a Systematic Review and Meta-analysis'. *BMC Public Health*, 20, 879.

Fardouly, J. and Vartanian, L. R. (2016) 'Social Media and Body Image Concerns: Current Research and Future Directions'. *Current Opinion in Psychology*, 9, 1–5.

Feather, J. (2006) *A History of British Publishing, Second Edition*. London: Routledge.

Fernandez, M. and Wilding, F. (2003) 'Situating Cyberfeminism''. In Maria Fernandez, Faith Wilding, and Michelle M. Wright (eds.), *Domain Errors! Cyberfeminist Practices*. New York: Autonomedia, 17–28.

Finley, L. and Esposito, L. (2020) 'The Immigrant as Bogeyman: Examining Donald Trump and the Right's Anti-immigrant, Anti-PC Rhetoric'. *Humanity & Society*, 44(2), 178–197.

Fitzsimmons, R. and Wilson, C. A. (eds.) (2020) *Beyond the Blockbusters: Themes and Trends in Contemporary Young Adult Fiction*. University Press of Mississippi.

Flood, A. (2020) '#Publishingpaidme: Authors Share Advances to Expose Racial Disparities'. *The Guardian* [online], 8 June. www.theguardian .com/books/2020/jun/08/publishingpaidme-authors-share-advances-to-expose-racial-disparities. Accessed 15th November 2023.

Flores, T. (2021) 'Latinidad Is Cancelled': Confronting an Anti-black Construct'. *Latin American and Latinx Visual Culture*, 3(3), 58–79.

Flowers, J. (2018) 'How Is It Okay to Be a Black Nerd?'. In K. Lane (ed.), *Age of the Geek: Depictions of Nerds and Geeks in Popular Media*, Houndmills: Palgrave Macmillan, 169–191.

Frank, A. P. (2001) 'Anthologies of Translation'. In M. Baker and K. Malmkjær (eds.), *Routledge Encyclopedia of Translation Studies*. New York: Routledge.

Gailey, A. (2020) 'Popular Poetry and the Rise of Anthologies'. In S. Belasco, T. S. Gaul, L. Johnson, and M. Soto (eds.), *A Companion to American Literature*, Hoboken: John Wiley & Sons, 133–147.

Galuszka, P. and Bystrov, V. (2014) 'The rise of fanvestors: A study of a crowdfunding community'. *First Monday*, 19(5). https://doi.org/10.5210/fm.v19i5.4117

Garretson, J. J. (2018) *The Path to Gay Rights: How Activism and Coming Out Changed Public Opinion*. Oxford: Oxford University Press.

Gates, H. (1992). *Loose Canons: Notes on the Culture Wars*. Oxford: Oxford University Press.

Gehring, D. and Wittkower, D. E. (2015) 'On the Sale of Community in Crowdfunding: Questions of Power, Inclusion, and Value'. In L. Bennett, B. Chin, and B. Jones (eds.), *Crowdfunding the Future: Media Industries, Ethics, and Digital* Societies, New York: Peter Lang, 65–79.

Germano, W. (2001) *Getting It Published, Third Edition*. Chicago: University of Chicago Press.

Gerson, G. (1989) 'Anthologies and the Canon of Early Canadian Women Writers'. In Lorraine McMullen (eds.), *Re(dis)covering Our Foremothers: Nineteenth-Century Canadian Women's Writers*, Ottawa: University of Ottawa Press, 55–76.

Gopinath, G. (2018) *Unruly Visions: The Aesthetic Practices of Queer Diaspora*. Durham: Duke University Press.

Gorak, J. (1991) *The Making of the Modern Canon: Genesis and Critic of a Literary Idea*. London: Athlone.

Grady, C. (2020) 'The controversy over the new immigration novel American Dirt, explained'. *VOX* [online]. www.vox.com/culture/2020/1/22/21075629/american-dirt-controversy-explained-jeanine-cummins-oprah-flatiron. Accessed 15th November 2023.

Green-Barteet, A. and Montz. Amy L. (2014) *Female Rebellion in Young Adult Dystopian Fiction*. Surrey: Ashgate, 33–50.

Grochowski, S. (2021) 'YA Anthologies Bring Diverse Voices Together'. *Publishers Weekly* [online]. www.publishersweekly.com/pw/by-topic/childrens/childrens-industry-news/article/86223-ya-anthologies-bring-diverse-voices-together.html. Accessed 15th November 2023.

Groesz, L. M., Levine, M. P., and Murnen, S. K. (2002) 'The Effect of Experimental Presentation of Thin Media Images on Body

Satisfaction: A Meta-analytic Review'. *International Journal of Eating Disorders*, 31(1), 1–16.

Grue, J. (2016) 'The Problem with Inspiration Porn: A Tentative Definition and a Provisional Critique'. *Disability & Society*, 31(6), 838–849.

Guillory, J. (1993) *Cultural Capital: The Problem of Literary Canon Formation*. Chicago: University of Chicago Press.

Haase, D. (2010) 'Decolonizing Fairy-Tale Studies'. *Marvels & Tales*, 24(1), 17–38.

Hafez, S. (1992) 'The Modern Arabic Short Story'. In M. M. Badawi (ed.), *Modern Arabic Literature*, Cambridge: Cambridge University Press, 270–328.

Hall, A. (2015) *Literature and Disability*. Abingdon: Routledge.

Hanson, C. (1989) *Re-reading the Short Story*. London: Palgrave Macmillan.

Henderson, A. (2021) 'Playing with Genre and Queer Narrative in the Novels of Malinda Lo'. *The International Journal of Young Adult Literature*, 2(1), 1–17.

Hopkins, D. (2008) 'On Anthologies'. *The Cambridge Quarterly*, 37(3), 285–304.

House of Commons Health and Social Care Committee (2022) 'The impact of body image on mental and physical health'. *Parliament UK*, 19 July. https://committees.parliament.uk/publications/23284/documents/170077/default. Accessed 15th November 2023.

Hudson, D. (ed.) (1956) *Modern English Short Stories 1930–1955*. London: Oxford University Press.

Hunter, A. (2007). *The Cambridge Introduction to the Short Story in English*. Cambridge: Cambridge University Press.

Imarisha, W., Brown, A. M., and Thomas, S. R. (eds.) (2015) *Octavia's Brood: Science Fiction Stories from Social Justice Movements*. Chico: A. K. Press.

Jarrell, R. (1994) 'Stories'. In C. E. May (ed.), *The New Short Story Theories*. Athens: Ohio University Press, 3–14.

Jenkins, B. (2020) 'Marginalization within Nerd Culture: Racism and Sexism within Cosplay'. *The Popular Culture Studies Journal*, 7(2), 157–174.

Jenkins, C. (1998) 'From Queer to Gay and Back Again: Young Adult Novels with Gay/Lesbian/Queer Content, 1969– 1997'. *The Library Quarterly: Information, Community, Policy*, 68(3), 298–334.

Jenkins, C. and Cart, M. (2018) *Representing the Rainbow in Young Adult Literature: LGBTQ+ Content since 1989*. Lanham: Rowman & Littlefield.

Jenkins, H. (2012) 'Superpowered Fans: The Many Worlds of San Diego's Comic- Con'. *Boom: A Journal of California*, 2(2), 22–36.

Jenny Brown Associates (2004) 'The Short Story in the UK'. The Short Story in the UK [online]. www.theshortstory.org.uk/aboutus/ The_Short_Story_in_the_UK_Report.pdf.

Jensen, K. (2020) '(Wh)Y A(n) Anthology: On the Rise and Reach of YA Anthologies'. *Book Riot* [online], 3 Feb. https://bookriot.com/ya-anthologies/. Accessed 15th November 2023.

Johnson, B. K. (1997) *Coming Out Every Day: Gay, Bisexual, or Questioning Man's Guide*. Oakland: New Harbinger.

Kaplan, C. and Rose, E. C. (1996). *The Canon and the Common Readers*. Knoxville: University of Tennessee Press.

Kaveney, R. (2012) 'Dark Fantasy and Paranormal Romance'. In E. James and F. Mendelsohn (eds.), *The Cambridge Companion to Fantasy Literature*, Cambridge: Cambridge University Press, 214–223.

Kidd, K. (1998) 'Introduction: Lesbian/Gay Literature for Children and Young Adults'. *Children's Literature Association Quarterly*, 23(3), 114–119.

Kilcup, K. L. (2000) 'Anthologizing Matters: The Poetry and Prose of Recovery Work'. *Symplokē*, 8(1/2), 36–56.

Kopyciok, S. and Silver, H. (2021) 'Left-Wing Xenophobia in Europe'. *Frontiers in Sociology*, 6, 666–717.

Kost, C. and Jamie, K. (2023) '"It Has Literally Been a Lifesaver": The Role of "Knowing Kinship" in Supporting Fat Women to Navigate Medical Fatphobia'. *Fat Studies*, 12(2), 311–324.

LaCapra, D. (2001) *Writing History, Writing Trauma*. Baltimore: John Hopkins University Press.

Lacey, T. (2000) 'The Anthology Problem: A Publisher's View'. In Barbara Korte, Ralf Schneider, and Stefanie Lethbridge (eds.), *Anthologies of British Poetry*, Leiden: Brill, 333–342.

Lai, L. (2020) 'Familiarizing Grist Village: Why I Write Speculative Fiction'. *Canadian Literature*, 240, 19–40.

Lau Ee Jia, L. (2003) 'Equating Womanhood with Victimhood: The Positionality of Women Protagonists in the Contemporary Writings of South Asian Women'. *Women's Studies International Forum*, 26(4), 369–378.

Lauter, P. (1991) *Canons and Contexts*. Oxford: Oxford University Press.
   (2004) 'Taking Anthologies Seriously'. *Melus*, 29(3–4), 19–39.

Lea, R. (2015) 'JK Rowling inspires surge to fund book on race and immigration in three days'. *The Guardian* [online], 3 December. www.theguardian.com/books/2015/dec/03/jk-rowling-david-nicholls-among-sponsors-crowdfunding-book-on-uk-race-and-immigration. Accessed 15th November 2023.

Lefevere, A. (1992) *Translation, Rewriting, and the Manipulation of Literary Fame: Translation Studies*. London: Routledge.

legislation.gov.uk (1998) 'Local Government Act 1988: Section 28'. www.legislation.gov.uk/ukpga/1988/9/section/28/enacted. Accessed 15th November 2023.

Lem, E. and Hassel, H. (2012) '"Killer" Katniss and "Lover Boy" Peeta: Suzanne Collins's Defiance of Gender-Genred Reading'. In M. F. Pharr and L. A. Clark (eds.), *Of Bread, Blood and the Hunger Games: Critical Essays on the Suzanne Collins Trilogy*, Jefferson: McFarland, 118–127.

Lu H. J. & Steele C. K. (2019) '"Joy Is Resistance": Cross-Platform Resilience and (Re)Invention of Black Oral Culture Online'. *Information, Communication & Society*, 22(6), 823–837.

Lyttle, S. (2022) 'Challenging the Love Triangle in Twenty-First-Century Fantastic Young Adult Literature'. *The International Journal of Young Adult Literature*, 3(1), 1–19.

MacLean, G. (1994) 'Literacy, Class, and Gender in Restoration England'. *Text*, 7, 307–335.

Macmillan (2023) 'Wild Tongues Can't Be Tamed'. *Macmillan*. https://academic.macmillan.com/academictrade/9781250763426/wildton guescantbetamed. Accessed 15th November 2023.

Mady, S., Biswas, D., Dadzie, C. A., Hill, R. P., & Paul, R. (2023). '"A Whiter Shade of Pale": Whiteness, Female Beauty Standards, and Ethical Engagement Across Three Cultures'. *Journal of International Marketing*, 31(1), 69–89.

Malcolm, D. (2012) *The British and Irish Short Story Handbook*. Oxford: Wiley Blackwell Literature.

Mann, B. (2009) 'Vampire Love: The Second Sex Negotiates the Twenty-first Century'. In William Irwin, J. Jeremy Wisnewski, and Rebecca House (eds.), *Twilight and Philosophy: Vampires, Vegetarians, and the Pursuit of Immortality*. Hoboken: John Wiley and Sons, 131–146.

March-Russell, P. (2009) *The Short Story: An Introduction*. Edinburgh: Edinburgh University Press.

March-Russell, P. and Awadalla, M. (2013) *The Postcolonial Short Story: Contemporary Essays*. Basingstoke: Palgrave Macmillan.

Mason, D. (2021) *Queer Anxieties of Young Adult Literature and Culture*. Jackson: Mississippi University Press.

Maton, K. I., Seidman, E., and Aber, M. S. (2011) 'Empowering Settings and Voices for Social Change: An Introduction'. In M. S. Aber, K. I. Maton, and E. Seidman (eds.), *Empowering Settings and Voices for Social Change*. Oxford: Oxford University Press, 1–11.

Matos, A. D. (2021) *The Reparative Possibilities of Queer Young Adult Literature and Culture*. New York: Routledge

McKenzie, D. F. (2002) 'The Book as an Expressive Form'. In David Finkelstein and Alistair McCleery (eds.), *The Book History Reader*, New York: Routledge, 27–38.

Meier, E. P. and Gray, J. (2014) 'Facebook Photo Activity Associated with Body Image Disturbance in Adolescent Girls'. *Cyberpsychology, Behavior, and Social Networking*, 17, 199–206.

Mental Health Foundation (2019) 'Body image report'. *Mental Health Foundation*. www.mentalhealth.org.uk/sites/default/files/2022-08/Body%20Image%20-%20How%20we%20think%20and%20feel%20about%20our%20bodies.pdf. Accessed 15th November 2023.

Mohammed, F. (2019) 'The business of the romance novel'. *JSTOR Daily*, 11 February 2019. https://daily.jstor.org/the-business-of-the-romance-novel/. Accessed 15th November 2023.

Montz, A. L. (2012) 'Costuming the Resistance: The Female Spectacle of Rebellion'. In Mary F. Pharr and Leisa A. Clark (eds.), *Of Bread, Blood, and the Hunger Games: Critical Essays on the Suzanne Collins Trilogy*, North Carolina: McFarland, 139–147.

Moses, T. (2009) 'Self-Labeling and Its Effects among Adolescents Diagnosed with Mental Disorders'. *Social Science & Medicine*, 68, 570–578.

Mourlane, S. (2023) 'In pushing away migrants, Giorgia Meloni forgets there was also a time when Italians weren't welcome'. *The*

Conversation, 19 January, https://theconversation.com/in-pushing-away-migrants-giorgia-meloni-forgets-there-was-also-a-time-when-italians-werent-welcome-197313. Accessed 15th November 2023.

Mujica, B. (1997) 'Teaching Literature: Canon, Controversy, and the Literary Anthology'. *Hispania*, 80(2), 203–215.

Mukherjee, R. and Banet-Weiser, S. (eds.) (2012) *Commodity Activism: Cultural Resistance in Neoliberal Times*. New York: New York University Press.

Nicholson, A. (2012) *Fighting to Serve: Behind the Scenes in the War to Repeal 'Don't Ask, Don't Tell'*. Chicago: Chicago Review Press.

Nilsen, A. P. and Donelson, K. L. (2009) *Literature for Today's Young Adults*. London: Pearson.

Norrick, R. C. (2018) 'Short Story Collections (and Cycles) in the British Literary Marketplace'. In Patrick Gill and Florian Kläger (eds.), *Constructing Coherence in the British Short Story Cycle*, Houndsmills: Routledge, 45–67.

Ochoa, M. (2022) 'Stop using 'Latinx' if you really want to be inclusive'. *The Conversation*, 9 September. https://theconversation.com/stop-using-latinx-if-you-really-want-to-be-inclusive-189358. Accessed 15th November 2023.

Orsini, F. (2004) 'India in the Mirror of World Fiction'. In Prendergast C. (ed.), *Debating World Literature*. London: Verso, 319–333.

Pace, B. G. (1992) ''The Textbook Canon: Genre, Gender, and Race in US Literature Anthologies'. *The English Journal*, 81(5), 33–38.

Paradies, Y. B., Denson, J., Elias, N., Priest, A., Pieterse, A. (2015) 'Racism as a Determinant of Health: A Systematic Review and Meta-analysis'. *PLoS One*, 10(9), e0138511.

Pattee, A. (2010) *Reading the Adolescent Romance: Sweet Valley High and the Popular Young Adult Romance Novel*. New York: Routledge.

Patterson, L. (1968) *Copyright in Historical Perspective*. Nashville: Vanderbilt University Press.

Patrick, D. and Reid, C. (2021) 'Is women's empowerment coming to publishing?'. *Publishers Weekly*, 29 January. www.publishersweekly.com/pw/by-topic/industry-news/publisher-news/article/85436-is-women-s-empowerment-coming-to-publishing.html. Accessed 15th November 2023.

Pearce, L., Fowler, C., Crawshaw, R. (eds.) (2013) *Postcolonial Manchester: Diaspora Space and the Devolution of Literary Culture*. Manchester: Manchester University Press.

Podos, R. (2019) [Twitter] 16th August. https://mobile.twitter.com/RebeccaPodos/status/1162421559308574728. Accessed 15th November 2023.

Power, C. (2011) 'Is the short story really the novel's poor relation'. *The Guardian* [online], 24 March. www.theguardian.com/books/booksblog/2011/mar/24/is-short-story-novel-poor-relation. Accessed 15th November 2023.

Pratt, M. L. (1994) 'The Short Story: The Long and Short of It'. In C. E. May (ed.), *The New Short Story Theories*, Athens: Ohio University Press, 91–114.

Pravinchandra, S. (2014). Not just Prose: The Calcutta Chromosome, the South Asian Short Story and the Limitations of Postcolonial Studies. *Interventions*, 16(3), 424–444.

Pravinchandra, S. (2018) 'Short Story and Peripheral Production'. In B. Etherington and J. Zimbler (eds.), *The Cambridge Companion to World Literature*. Cambridge: Cambridge University Press, 197–210.

Prescott, L. (2016) 'The Short Story Anthology: Shaping the Canon'. In D. Head (ed.), *The Cambridge History of the English Short Story*. Cambridge: Cambridge University Press, 564–580.

Preston, A. (2019) 'Refugee tales and migration – four books that help us understand a crisis'. *The Guardian*, 23 June. www.theguardian.com/books/2019/jun/23/refugee-tales-migration-books-ungrateful-refugee-our-city-dina-nayeri-jon-bloomfield-jonathan-portes. Accessed 15th November 2023.

Price, L. (2000) *The Anthology and the Rise of the Novel: From Richardson to George Eliot*. Cambridge: Cambridge University Press.

Publishers Association (2023) UK Publishing Workforce: Diversity, inclusion and belonging. Publishers Association. www.publishers.org.uk/wp-content/uploads/2023/01/The-UK-Publishing-Workforce-Diversity-Inclusion-and-Belonging-in-2022.pdf. Accessed 15th November 2023.

Rabinowitz, R. (2003) 'Fat Characters in Recent Young Adult Fiction'. *The Free Library* [online]. www.thefreelibrary.com/Fat+characters+in+recent+young+adult+fiction.-a0108266685.

Ramdarshan-Bold, M. (2018) 'The Eight Percent Problem: Authors of Colour in the British Young Adult Market (2006–2016)'. *Publishing Research Quarterly*, 34(3), 385–406.

    (2019a) *Inclusive Young Adult Fiction: Authors of Colour in the United Kingdom*. London: Palgrave.

    (2019b) Representation of People of Colour among Children's Book Authors and Illustrators (2007–2017). BookTrust [online]. www.booktrust.org.uk/globalassets/resources/represents/booktrust-represents-diversity-childrens-authors-illustrators-report.pdf.

    (2021) 'The Thirteen Percent Problem: Authors of Colour in the British Young Adult Market, 2017–2019 Edition'. *The International Journal of Young Adult Literature*, 2(1), 1–35. www.ijyal.ac.uk/articles/10.24877/IJYAL.37

Richmond, K. J. (2018) *Mental Illness in Young Adult Literature: Exploring Real Struggles through Fictional Characters*. Santa Barbara, CA: ABC-CLIO.

Rodgers, R. F., Meyer, C., and McCaig, D. (2020) 'Characterizing a Body Positive Online Forum: Resistance and Pursuit of Appearance-Ideals'. *Body Image*, 33, 199–206.

Rodriguez Garcia, M., Heerma van Voss, L., & van Nederveen Meerkerk, E. J. V. (eds.) (2017) *Selling Sex in the City: A Global History of Prostitution, 1600s-2000s*. (Studies in Global Social History; Vol. 31). Leiden: Brill Academic Publishers. https://doi.org/10.1163/9789004346253

Roof, J. (1996) *Come as You Are: Sexuality and Narrative*. New York: Columbia University Press.

Sands-O'Connor, K. (2023) *Diversity and Inclusion in Young Adult Publishing, 1960–1980*. Cambridge: Cambridge University Press.

Saha, A. (2017) *Race and the Cultural Industries*. Cambridge: Polity Press.

Saha, A. and Van Lente, S. (2022) 'The Limits of Diversity: How Publishing Industries Make Race'. *International Journal of Communication*, 16, 1804–1822.

Salt (2023) 'Best British Short Stories'. *Salt*. www.saltpublishing.com/collections/best-british-short-stories/format-paperback. Accessed 15th November 2023.

Sánchez Prado, I. M. (2021) 'Commodifying Mexico: On American Dirt and the Cultural Politics of a Manufactured Bestseller'. *American Literary History*, 33(2), 371–393.

Sastre, A. (2014) 'Towards a Radical Body Positive: Reading the Online "Body Positive Movement"'. *Feminist Media Studies*, 14, 929–943.

Savin-Williams, R. C. (2001) 'A Critique of Research on Sexual Minority Youths'. *Journal of Adolescence*, 24, 5–13.

(2005) *The New Gay Teenager*. London: Harvard University Press.

Saxey, E. (2008) *Homoplot: The Coming-Out Story and Gay, Lesbian, and Bisexual Identity*. New York: Peter Lang .

Schmidt, S. (2019) 'A language for all, Un Lenguaje para todos'. *Washington Post*, 5 Dec. www.washingtonpost.com/dc-md-va/2019/12/05/teens-argentina-are-leading-charge-gender-neutral-language/. Accessed 15th November 2023.

Schouler-Ocak, M., Bhugra, D., Kastrup, M., et al. (2021) 'Racism and Mental Health and the Role of Mental Health Professionals'. *EuropeanPsychiatry*, 64(1), E42.

Seidman, S. (2002) *Beyond the Closet: The Transformation of Gay and Lesbian Life*. New York: Routledge.

Shapiro, L. (2021) 'Blurbed to death how one of publishing's most hyped books became its biggest horror story – and still ended up a best seller', *Vulture*, 5 Jan. www.vulture.com/article/american-dirt-jeanine-cummins-book-controversy.html. Accessed 15th November 2023.

Sher, R. B. (2006) *The Enlightenment and the Book: Scottish Authors and Their Publishers in Eighteenth-Century Britain, Ireland, and America*. Chicago: The University of Chicago Press.

Simpson, J. (2020) 'Silence and Absence in the Political. Discourse on Section 28 and Children's Literature in the United Kingdom'. *Barnbroken: The Journal of Children's Literature Research*, 43, 1–17.

 (2021) *Section 28 Then and Now: A Tripartite Investigation into Narratives of Sexuality, Gnder, and the Role of Fiction for Children and Young People in Shaping LGBT+ Exclusion and Inclusion* (Doctoral thesis, The University of Strathclyde). https://stax.strath.ac.uk/concern/theses/w95050945

So, R. (2020) *Redlining Culture: A Data History of Racial Inequality and Postwar Fiction*. New York: Columbia University Press.

Sobande, F. (2021) 'Spectacularized and Branded Digital (Re)presentations of Black People and Blackness'. *Television & New Media*, 22(2), 131–146.

Sohn, S. H. (2019) 'Defining and Exploring Asian American Speculative Fiction'. *Oxford Research Encyclopedia of Literature*, https://doi.org/10.1093/acrefore/9780190201098.013.870. Accessed 15th November 2023.

Srivastava, N. (2010) 'Anthologizing the Nation: Literature Anthologies and the Idea of India'. *Journal of Postcolonial Writing*, 46(2), 151–163.

Stemp, J. (2004) 'Devices and Desires: Science Fiction, Fantasy and Disability in Literature for Young People'. *Disability Studies Quarterly*, 24(1).

Strings, S. (2019) *Fearing the Black Body: The Racial Origins of Fat Phobia*. New York: NYU Press.

Sullivan, M. K. (2003) *Sexual Minorities: Discrimination, Challenges and Development in America*. New York: Routledge.

Taylor, D. (2023) '"Draconian" migration bill could leave tens of thousands destitute or locked up'. *The Guardian* [online], 22 March. www.theguardian.com/world/2023/mar/22/draconian-migration-bill-could-leave-tens-of-thousands-destitute-or-locked-up#:~:text=The%20bill%20promises%20to%20clamp,seeking%20asylum%20from%20the%20country. Accessed 15th November 2023.

Thompson, J. K., Herbozo, S. M., Himes, S. M., Yamamiya, Y. (2005) 'Weight-Related Teasing in Adults'. In K. D. Brownell, R. M. Puhl, M. B. Schwartz, L. Rudd (eds.), *Weight Bias: Nature Consequences, and Remedies*, New York: Guilford Press, 137–149.

Toliver, S. R. (2020) 'Can I Get a Witness? Speculative Fiction as Testimony and Counterstory'. *Journal of Literacy Research*, 52(4), 507–529.

Thomas, E. E. (2019) *The Dark Fantastic: Race and the Imagination from "Harry Potter" to "The Hunger Games"*. New York: NYU Press.

Truman, S. E. (2019) 'SF! Haraway's Situated Feminisms and Speculative Fabulations in English Class'. *Studies in Philosophical Education*, 38, 31–42.

Verea, M. (2018) 'Anti-immigrant and Anti-Mexican Attitudes and Policies during the First 18 Months of the Trump Administration'. *Norteamérica*, 13(2), 197–226. https://doi.org/10.22201/cisan.24487228e.2018.2.335

Wakholi, P. M. (2017) 'Cultural Activism and the Arts: Cultural Memory, Identity, and Community Building'. *International Journal of Social, Political & Community Agendas in the Arts*, 12(3), 21–39.

Wallace, S., Nazroo, J., Bécares, L. (2016) 'Cumulative Effect of Racial Discrimination on the Mental Health of Ethnic Minorities in the United Kingdom'. *American Journal of Public Health*, 106(7), 1294–1300.

Whitt, J. E. (2022). 'Introduction: Lgbt Soldiers in Military History'. *International Journal of Military History and Historiography*, 42(1), 7–18.

Wickens, C. M. (2011) 'Codes, Silences, and Homophobia: Challenging Normative Assumptions about Gender and Sexuality in Contemporary LGBTQ Young Adult Literature'. *Children's Literature in Education*, 42(2), 148–164.

Williams, M. Sutherland, A., Roy-Chowdhury, V. et al. (2023) 'The Effect of the Brexit Vote on the Variation in Race and Religious Hate Crimes in England, Wales, Scotland and Northern Ireland'. *The British Journal of Criminology*, 63(4), 1003–1023. https://doi.org/10.1093/bjc/azac071.

Wilson, J. (2020) 'White nationalist hate groups have grown 55% in Trump era, report finds'. *The Guardian*, 18 March. www.theguardian.com/world/2020/mar/18/white-nationalist-hate-groups-southern-poverty-law-center. Accessed 15th November 2023.

Young, S. (2012) 'We're not here for your inspiration'. *ABC News*, 3 Jul. www.abc.net.au/news/2012-07-03/young-inspiration-porn/4107006. Accessed 15th November 2023.

Young Women's Trust (2019) 'Young Women's Feminism and Activism 2019'. *Young Women's Trust*. www.youngwomenstrust.org/wp-con tent/uploads/2020/11/Young-womens-feminism-and-activism-2019-report.pdf. Accessed 15th November 2023.

Yu, P. (2018) 'Poems in Their Place: Collections and Canons in Early Chinese Literature'. In Paul W. Kroll (ed.), *Critical Readings on Tang China Volume 2*. Leiden: Brill, 936–966.

Cambridge Elements ☰

Publishing and Book Culture

SERIES EDITOR
Samantha Rayner
University College London

Samantha Rayner is Professor of Publishing and Book Cultures
at UCL. She is also Director of UCL's Centre for Publishing,
co-Director of the Bloomsbury CHAPTER (Communication
History, Authorship, Publishing, Textual Editing and
Reading) and co-Chair of the Bookselling Research Network.

ASSOCIATE EDITOR
Leah Tether
University of Bristol

Leah Tether is Professor of Medieval Literature and Publishing
at the University of Bristol. With an academic background in
medieval French and English literature and a professional
background in trade publishing, Leah has combined her
expertise and developed an international research profile in
book and publishing history from manuscript to digital.

About the Series

This series aims to fill the demand for easily accessible, quality texts available for teaching and research in the diverse and dynamic fields of Publishing and Book Culture. Rigorously researched and peer-reviewed Elements will be published under themes, or 'Gatherings'. These Elements should be the first check point for researchers or students working on that area of publishing and book trade history and practice: we hope that, situated so logically at Cambridge University Press, where academic publishing in the UK began, it will develop to create an unrivalled space where these histories and practices can be investigated and preserved.

Cambridge Elements ☰

Publishing and Book Culture

YOUNG ADULT PUBLISHING
Gathering Editor: Melanie Ramdarshan Bold
Melanie Ramdarshan Bold is Senior Lecturer in Children's
Literature and Literacies in the School of Education at the
University of Glasgow, where she teaches and researches topics
related to Children's and Young Adult literature and book
culture. Her main research interest centres on developments in
authorship, publishing, and reading, and inclusiveness and
representation in literary culture, with a focus on books for
children and young adults.

ELEMENTS IN THE GATHERING

Printed in the United States
by Baker & Taylor Publisher Services